CW00719629

Top:THE FIGHTER COLLECTION P-38 *was photographed on an air test out of Chino, California by* **Frank Mormillo** *just weeks ago.*
Bottom: Norman Pealing *captured the Alpine Fighter Collection's F4U-1A Birdcage Corsair Bu17995 (ex N90285) that was imported in to New Zealand and registered as ZK-FUI last year. Warbirds Worldwide member Keith Skilling is at the controls.*

O P I N I O N

In many ways this latest edition of Warbirds Worldwide marks a departure for us. Thanks to Mark Sheppard and Axel Urbanke we are able to cover the amazing recovery of a Fw190 from Lake Schwerin. The aircraft is so rare and recognisable that I felt it deserved space in our publication. But this is not the only reason. I think that with the supply of warbirds from foreign air arms starting to reach exhaustion point, and the thirst for rarer types and greater restoration challenges we will begin to turn to the forests and the lakes, the desert, tundra and wasteland to an even greater degree than ever before. We have already seen significant finds in Russia, and we know there is feverish activity in these regions. I am taking the advice of one of this countries leading collectors - WW will wait and see rather than make any assumptions as to what is coming out and where it is going. Suffice to say the talk is exciting and shows great promise for the future. Let's hope the resources can be and will be made available to get these fine aircraft back in the air. Otherwise I think we might just as well have left them where they were.

Just a few weeks ago I was asked, in the light of the current recession if I felt warbird prices and the market in general had collapsed. As a non-owner I do not have a vested interest in prices moving skywards, but I certainly do not believe the warbird market is big enough to collapse. The majority of owners seem to be owners for the pleasure of ownership and the enjoyment of flying warbirds rather than for short term investment. There has been a small drop off in reported activity, but in general aircraft are moving in private circles and the majority of owners are optimistic. Some have had to sell as a result of other effects of the recession, and as a result of quick sales the prices has been reflected thus. I do not believe there is any parallel with the classic car market in any way shape or form. Basically, there has never been a better time to buy warbirds, to make that long term investment, hopefully for long term enjoyment!

Another victory for the keep 'em flying brigade is the increasing number of warbirds being taken out of museums and removed from exposed pylons - like the Spitfire in the Netherlands that has just been replaced by the fibreglass replica - see the above photograph-in order to provide raw material for restoration to flying condition. This is encouraging and we wish the Dutch Spitfire Flight the best of luck with their second aircraft (Mk IX MK959). It is refreshing to see the majority of national collections taking advantage of the skill of private operators in negotiating new types to enhance static collections all over the world. If one does not exist perhaps we should establish an international museum exchange programme so that the huge numbers of aircraft currently held

in store away from the public gaze (whether it is in a national collection or a private collection the majority are of these are at least visible) can be exchanged with other collections or private individuals. It is my strong belief that private enterprise can be made to work hand in hand with national collections. It is also my personal opinion that defence agencies should, if they wish, sell to the highest bidder, particularly where taxpayers money is involved, and however the disposal is made.

We are witness to some exciting prospects for the 1991 show season, and already two leading warbird shows are at the advanced planning stage. Wanaka in New Zealand will see another high class air show, which reflects the amount of energy injected into it by organiser Tim Wallis of the Alpinedeer Group/Alpine Fighter Collection. Held over the Easter weekend it is set to be a stunner! You can read about it in the Warbirds Airnews section.

At home in the UK the Classic Fighter Air Display is also shaping up nicely. I would strongly recommend supporting all the warbird

events, or as many as your pocket will allow. The CFAD organisers have set an excellent value for money price, particularly with advance ticket sales. See Page 32.

On the subject of air displays the Association of Air Display Organisers and Participants are in the process of reforming themselves into the European Air Display Association. This forward looking body will no doubt represent British views on the European scene and hopefully attract some European participation.We say thanks and keep up the good work!

Last but not least, hats off to the Old Flying Machine Company for their efforts in transporting the Me109J out to New Zealand for the Wanaka show. We had reported on this particular organisation's record of attending overseas airshows before but this must be a new milestone in international cooperation. We wish them all the best and successful dogfighting at Wanaka. I'm handing over the editorial to Butch Schroeder in WW21, so cheers for now! **WW Paul Coggan**

WARBIRDS
W O R L D W I D E
Volume Five Number Four
FOUNDERS:
Paul A. Coggan
John R. Sandberg
Henry J. Schroeder III

EDITORIAL
Editorial Director/Publisher: Paul A. Coggan

Editorial Address: P.O. Box 99., Mansfield,
Notts NG19 9GU, ENGLAND
Tel: (0623) 24288 Fax(0623) 22659

Design Consultant: John M. Dibbs

Company Secretary: Amanda E. Coggan BA

Financial Adviser: Philip S. Warner F.C.A.

Chief Pilot
Mark Hanna (Old Flying Machine Co.)

Contributors:
Peter Anderson (Australia)
Gary Brown (UK)
Joe Cupido (USA)
Robert DeGroat (USA)
John Dibbs (UK)
Christophe Donnet (Switzerland)
Jeffrey Ethell (USA)
Jeremy K. Flack (UK)
Erich Gandet (Switzerland)
Alan Gruening (USA)
James Kightly (UK)
Philip Makanna (USA)
Frank Mormillo (USA)
Dick Phillips (USA)
Sharon Sandberg (USA)
Mark Sheppard (UK)
Michael Shreeve (UK)
Chuck Sloat (Canada)
Eddie Toth (USA)
Richard Winslade (UK)

SUBSCRIPTION INFORMATION

UK £18.00, Rest of Europe £20.00, USA $44.00, Canada $C48.00, Australia $A49.00, New Zealand NZ$59.00 Hong Kong £20.00. We accept **VISA, MASTERCARD, AMEX & DINERS**.Please send fee to above address or Fax credit card details to (0623) 22659 telling us which copy you wish to start with. Copies sent airmail overseas in card envelopes.

C O N T E N T S

The scene at Shoreham when the first ex Mozambique Harvard was rolled out (see Page 43) Left to right Andrew Edie, rock star Gary Numan and John Woodhouse **(Photograph by C. Warner)**

6 KALAMAZOO THUNDERBOLT
Gerard Pahl of the *Kalamazoo Aviation History Museum* in Kalamazoo, Michigan, writes about the recovery (from Peru) and restoration of their Republic P-47.

16 RUSSIAN THUNDER
Rock Star *Gary Numan* flies Eddie Coventry's Yak-11 G-OYAK from Duxford and enthuses about its fighter like performance. Photography by *John Dibbs.*

18 *WING TO WING*
Darton International's David Clinton explains the finer points of formation flying and outlines plans for an exciting new film on the subject.

25 SUPERB SABRE
Paul Coggan researches the history of the *Golden Apple Trust's* F-86A N178 recently arrived in the UK and set to thrill enthusiasts all over the country.

29 HELLCAT UPDATE
Michael Shreeve updates us on the latest Hellcat happenings and produces a listing of the current known survivors around the world. Exclusive photography by *John Dibbs*

34 BOB POND'S PRACTICAL WARBIRD
Frank Mormillo writes from Chino, California and *Fighter Rebuilders* where a huge multi-seat Skyraider is proving to be a practical warbird.

43 MOZAMBIQUE HARVARD
Philip Warner reports from Shoreham, on the roll out of the first of several ex Mozambique AF Harvards. *John Dibbs* took the pictures

55 LAKE SCHWERIN'S DORA NINE
Mark Sheppard collaborates with *Axel Urbanke* to produce this fascinating insight into the recovery of an Fw190 from Lake Schwerin.

■ Warbirds Airnews P11 ■ CLASSIC FIGHTER AIR DISPLAY Shapes UP P32 ■ Vintage Props & Jets P38 ■ Good Fortune & Jet Warbirds P40 ■ C'est Magnifique - French Warbirds P48

WIN AN EASTMAN LEATHER CLOTHING G-2 P50.

Kalamazoo Thunderbolt

Gerard Pahl reports on the recovery of six Thunderbolts from Peru and the restoration of the Air Zoo's example.

The story began in the early 1970's when Ed Jurist of *Vintage Aircraft International Inc.* had been tipped off as to the presence of Thunderbolts in Peru by friends who were looking for pre-World War II automobiles. When he arrived at the Peruvian air force base in Piura to rescue the six Thunderbolts, including 49181, he had anticipated some problems but he had not fully realised what he had let himself in for. Indeed, his adventure would pale the likes of *Indiana Jones* and *James Bond*.

Not surprisingly, in countries where the unconventional is the conventional, Ed soon found himself enmeshed with a group of rogues who, for a price, could grease the skids putting him in touch with the right people to secure the aircraft.

The leader of these scoundrels was officer "S" (Mr. Jurist asked that the man's full name not be used for safety sake as he and his people are still powerful within the Peruvian hierarchy). Officer S's covert crew consisted of his brother, a Captain, another relative, a woman, and several other associates of ill repute. Considerable pressure was placed on Ed to sign various agreements which would be the groups *mordida* (bite) of the action. They called for shipment of two Cadillacs to Lima and the covert supply of money to a woman in Long Island on a weekly basis. Ed resisted, but time and again pressure was brought to bear. Feeling rather tense about these secret activities, Ed tried to work within the appropriate channels. Officer S became overbearing, turning the screw repeatedly. Finally, Ed blew up and told him that since officer S could not keep the promises he made, he would have nothing to do with the sordid group. Backing off, S relented and promised action by the following morning. Action was to come a little earlier than morning.

From the outset, things did not look right. The gang took Ed to a squalid *cantina*, the Peruvian equivalent of a greasy spoon. Officer S, his brother, and the olive skinned senorita were pleasant enough, but Ed felt as if he were on a razor's edge. With trepidation Ed ate - sparingly. He drank - sparingly. By midnight his stomach was churning and heart palpitating. This was not *Montezuma's Revenge*; he was certain he had been poisoned!

Rushed to a clinic in San Isidora he was revived only to be locked up on the sixth floor of a security ward. For all he knew they had thrown away the key. Desolate, Ed wondered if he would ever return to the U.S., let alone be lucky enough to stay alive.

Fortunately, the son of a well-to-do Peruvian family was in hospital with a broken leg and learned of the American sequestered in the security ward. Svec 'Pancho' Hartinger used his influence to see Ed, with whom he became closely acquainted. The two men formulated a scheme to gain the American's freedom. Though 'Pancho' would be searched when he left the wing, Ed was able to write a message to the American Embassy and conceal it in the plaster-cast surrounding the Peruvian's leg. Surreptitiously, the message was smuggled from the hospital and 'Pancho', with his English teacher wife Wendy, alerted the American authorities.

Released from his incarceration, Ed was able to legitimately put together a deal to acquire the aircraft. Though he was competing with five other individuals and two foreign governments, through the efforts of a General Piccone, a Dr.

Top: An ex Peruvian P-47 (FAP114 44-90471 later registered N47DA to the Military Aircraft Restoration Corp.)is off-loaded from the Rosaldina at Brownsville, Texas. Right: interestingly showing the last four digits of the construction number on the fin, this P-47D is ex FAP122 - now with Plane's of Fame East as N47RP (Courtesy Ed Jurist)

Grunewald, and State Department lawyers he secured the six Thunderbolts, had them broken down, crated, and shipped to the U.S. But his troubles were not over. Officer S was not about to let this *gringo* get away.

As Ed made his way through the Lima airport lobby, the mist of the *Garua* condensed on anything cool to touch. But more was sweating than just the stone walls. Ed warily passed the armed security guards at the loading gate and climbed the ramp into his awaiting *Lufthansa* jetliner. Relieved as he buckled the seat belt, Ed felt secure - he was heading home! With a flurry, soldiers rushed the plane, automatic weapons cocked. Grappling, they pulled Ed from his seat and rudely placed him under arrest. "Someone" had accused the American of being an industrial agent for *Price Waterhouse* and smuggling important Peruvian documents concerning the silver trade. Wrenched from the plane and searched, Ed was soon freed when it was obvious that he was not carrying such documents. Somewhat weather worn, he returned home.

Though it seemed all was in the clear, for a while Ed thought that 'S' had struck again. The P-47s and over 45 tons of spares had been loaded on to an ignominious scow called by the misnomer, *Rosaldina*. The ship had embarked for the U.S. from the port of Paita, but after passing through the Panama Canal, it looked as though the freighter had disappeared from the face of the earth. All efforts to locate the vessel failed with ship, crew and Thunderbolts, presumed lost at sea. Finally the freighter was found in a tiny port in the Gulf of Mexico having taken shelter there from a hurricane which had devastated the area. On September 5, 1969 the *Rosaldina* anchored in Brownsville, Texas and the planes were flatbedded to the *Confederate Air Force* in Harlingen for reassembly. Thunderbolt 49181 was not to fly, however, until August 28, 1972 and eventually found a home in California.

Les Friend of San Diego loved and babied his aeroplanes but when he bought the Thunderbolt from Dave Tallichet "it was really in awful shape". Dave had purchased the plane in '75 and let it sit for two years. Friend hired Dick Martin and Bill Yoak to put the P-47 into safe flying condition. Dick and Bill had to pull the whole belly out of it, replace all the hydraulics and electrical systems and install a supercharger, replacing the fuel pumps, carburettor, and the propeller. Friend flew the Thunderbolt on and off for the next two years until July 26, 1979. In that time he appeared at many air shows including a charity show to help pay the medical bills of a high school student,

Kip Hayes, who had been paralysed while playing football. In May, 1979 at the P-47 *Pilot's Association* Reunion in Chino, Les and the Thunderbolt thrilled hundreds of ex Jug jockeys, by flying in formation with Dave Tallichet's ex Peruvian N47DA. In 1979 the aircraft was taken to Camarillo, California for a dedication to Gabby Gabreski. "Gabby sat in the cockpit with tears in his eyes" said Les. This was not the first, nor the last time that Col. Frances Gabreski was to come into contact with the P-47 Thunderbolt...........

"A scorching flash seemed to penetrate the armour plate behind my head, searing it's way through helmet and skull. Instinctively, I yanked the stick to my gut, pushed hard left rudder and craned my neck to see what jumped us. As *Blue Flight Leader* I was escorting B-17s about 10 miles southeast of Oldenburg. *Blue Two* and I

had just begun our attack on some Bf.110s and I knew we had been bounced. Jerry had laid a trap and I fell for it.

As my Jug struggled to nose the sky again, a rain of fire and shards of metal pummelled the plane. In a split second I knew the sickening truth. Two '47s from my own flight had collided. Their pilots, over zealous to strike the enemy, had become careless.

Comprehending what had happened, my body automatically made the one decision available; resume the attack. Hurtling to 22,000 feet. I closed on the twin engine *Zerstorer*. The pilot had seen me and went into a gentle dive, but made no radical manoeuvres to avoid taking hits. And take hits he did. At about 700 yards I squeezed the trigger and the eight Brownings spit a fusillade of copper causing a sparkle of strikes on the starboard wing and engine. Intent on the kill, I closed, hammering away with my .50s when I realised I was flying right through the 110. Fortunately, the German aircraft exploded just before my T-bolt collided with it, yet my left wing was torn and the leading edge of the right was crushed. I had a few souvenirs to take home

that entered through the cockpit air intake. The windscreen was a bit on the greasy side too.

Lt. Gene Barnum, my wingman, was still with me and we climbed to the left of the bombers. I observed another 110 positioning for an attack to the rear of the Forts. Barnum and I Split-essed, pouncing on it at a terrific speed. The Luftwaffe pilot broke of his attack and made a diving turn to avoid our onslaught. Clocking 420 mph at 18,000 I was about to ram the drab plane, when I realised the quickening closure rate. At 600 yards, the guns torched again scoring hits at the wing root. Breaking my attack at 450 mph and 14,000 ft., I saw the *Destroyer* go straight in, smearing the earth in a boiling explosion of oily smoke and fire."

These were just two of the 31 victories scored by Col. Francis Gabreski as he flew through Fortress Europe's skies. The former Spitfire and Thunderbolt pilot was relating what it was like to fly in combat to a crowd of aviation enthusiasts at the *Kalamazoo Aviation History Museum*. As America's top ace in Europe and the highest scoring U.S. ace to survive World War II, Col. Gabreski went on to flame 6 1/2 Migs in Korea for a total of 37 1/2 kills. He is one of only five Air Force pilots to become a double Ace of Korea and World War II.

Now, at the age of 72 and the father of nine, Gabby happily visited his old comrade - in - arms, the P-47. Col. Gabreski came to see the *Air Zoo's* Thunderbolt which carries the paint scheme of the 'craft he flew in the 61st Fighter Squadron, 56th Fighter Group, 8th Air Force. The reunion took place May 11 and 12 1991 to celebrate the 50th Anniversary of the First Flight of the XP-47B (May 6, 1941) Hundreds of people met Colonel Gabreski and were treated to the thrill of seeing and feeling the *Air Zoo's* Thunderbolt fly. (When it roars overhead, just above the museum's roof, the P&W R-2800 reverberates in your chest!)

Vlado Lenoch horsed his blue nose P-51D, *Moonbeam McSwine* through the sun burnt sky to join '47 pilot, Lan Wright, entertaining the crowd with twin take offs and echelon passes. Programmes were given by history professor, Richard Cahow, on the Evolution of the P-47 and the former editor of *Thunderbolt Enthusiast*, Tim Savage, on Surviving Thunderbolts.

To remember the Golden Jubilee, a commemorative postcard was printed with New Mexico artist Peter L. Bilan designing a special cancellation which was issued by the U.S. Postal Service. Vintage USA Air Mail stamps, collected by philatelist Bob Baker, were placed

on the cards. Also, aviation artist George Sperl showed his work during the affair.

It was along road to be travelled before this momentous event celebrating the 50th anniversary of the Thunderbolt both generally and for this aeroplane specifically. One might suggest that this classic aircraft started out as a Russian aeroplane! This consummate fighter was the culmination of two geniuses of the aeronautical engineering world, Alexander Seversky and Alexander Kartveli, both of whom were expatriated Russians who had emigrated to the U.S. because of the Bolshevik revolution.

Seversky's and Kartveli's first big thrust into the aviation manufacturing business was a response to the 1935 competition for a new Army Air Corps (AAC) pursuit plane. Through various design changes and up-gradings, the P-35 was born. This aircraft carried two .50 and two .30 calibre machine guns. It had a range of some 400 miles greater than it's competitors and three times greater than the AAC's then current pursuit, the P-26 Peashooter. Yet, this contemporary of the Spitfire, Hurricane, Zero and Messerschmitt showed poorly in early World War II combat. Of the 48 machines assigned to the Philippines, only eight remained after two days of hostilities.

The design, however, eventually evolved through the P-41, P-43 and AP-10 to a plane which would ultimately be named Thunderbolt, the largest and heaviest single seat, single engine, piston driven production fighter ever built. Ironically, this radial engine eight gun monolith (19,400 lbs loaded) was the answer to AAC Circular Proposal (39-770) of August,1939 which called for a new pursuit plane which was small in size(4,900 lbs. gross weight), powered

by an Allison V-1710, and armed with two .50 calibre machine guns!

What had happened between conception and final product was Hitler's invasion of Poland, the beginning of World War II. Experience in the field showed that the original specifications for the aircraft were clearly insufficient. New specs were drawn which included: higher ceiling and turbo-supercharging, escort abilities, heavy firepower and armour, greater range than an

Top: The Air Zoo's newly acquired P-47D still in Les Friend's paint scheme (Bill Painter). This particular P-47D is ex FAP115,N47DC, N159LF (Les Friend) and is now N444SU. Lower: Colonel Francis Gabreski, top scoring U.S. ace in Europe during World War II. Note how each kill mark has a stencilled aircraft type beneath it! (Photo courtesy Col. Gabreski).

interceptor, level speed of 400 mph, and maximum manoeuvrability. The P-47 delivered all of these and more.

A legend in air to air combat, all variants of the Thunderbolt were noted for their massive fire power and extreme durability. In a one second burst of all eight guns, 14 pounds of lead would be travelling toward their target at muzzle velocity of 2,850 ft/second and could strike that target from a distance of 3,500ft. Eventually this bomber escort was to become one of the most devastating ground attack vehicles during the war. Large in size, larger in protection, it was also the pursuit plane produced in the largest number of any U.S. fighter.

With such a history in development and use, it was only natural that the fledgling *Kalamazoo Air Zoo* would want such an aircraft and in 1979 it had the opportunity to take a specific Thunderbolt, 49181, and put it back into pristine condition. When *Air Zoo* Executive Director Bob Ellis and President Sue Parish visited Les Friend about acquiring the aircraft, it was in fairly good shape. Bob and Sue were impressed with what they saw and purchased the plane for the *Kalamazoo Aviation History Museum.* Randy Sohn ferried the aircraft to Oshkosh in 1979 where it caused quite a stir with several people climbing all over the Jug almost as it taxied off the runway. Thunderbolts were and still are rare aircraft to see at airshows. It was then taken to Kalamazoo.

The Thunderbolt made a few familiarisation flights that fall, but was soon grounded so it could go through a complete restoration and be a shining example of all of the Thunderbolts that went before it. However, it would be two years before the work would begin as the *Air*

Zoo's staff was, at that time elbow deep in restoration of the museum's Grumman Hellcat. The restoration was anticipated to be fairly straightforward and in many respects, it was. Still when you disassemble a 40 year old aircraft, you are bound to find some surprises, and this *Jug* was full of them.

The initial objective was to restore the machine with all it's systems in perfect working order. It was completely dismantled; wings demated, hydraulics and electrics removed, and the Pratt & Whitney sent away for overhaul. Anything that could be unbolted and removed was. Up cropped trouble. According to Dick Schaus, museum A&P/IA (FAA Inspection Authorization), there was a problem with the push-pull mechanism which runs from the stick to the elevator.

Evidently , at some period in the life of the aircraft, this mechanism had been over stressed causing cracks in the rivetted joints between the rod ends and the control tubes. In subsequent use if the stick had been yanked too hard, the resulting stress might have caused the tubes to fail with a resultant loss of elevator control. Though easily resolved, the problem was not something that could have been identified during a routine annual inspection. The plane is called the *Jug* because of it's milk bottle shape, but it is very cramped in the tail of the fuselage due to the 250lb. turbocharger. Since access is so limited, normally the push-pull tubes could be examined at a distance but not closely inspected. In this complete restoration, however, the turbine was dropped making a close inspection easier and more thorough.

The turbocharger itself was rebuilt according to specs. The restoration team, though, had to literally manufacture specialised tools for the project. After removing the charger, the 'biggie' showed up: it appears that at some time it blew up! Not in combat, but of its own accord. Essentially, a turbocharger is an air pump designed to deliver pressurised air to the engine so it can operate in the thin air at high altitude. It is driven by the pilot who remotely adjusts the aperture of the wastegates in the side of the fuselage. At low level operation, the turbocharger could overspeed and literally tear itself apart, explosively. This evidently is what had happened.

Indications of the disintegration showed in the repairs done to the aft portion of the fuselage as it appeared the stringers had been severed and cracked then mended and extensive sheet metal work had been done. Two years after the restoration, because of maintenance and safety concerns, it was decided the the turbocharger system would be deactivated. To accomplish this, spare wastegates, modified to dump all of the exhaust, were installed. Yet, the aircraft is still fairly original. In fact putting the turbocharger back on line would be quite a simple matter. Performance of the Thunderbolt has

*Top: Air Zoo President Sue Parish taxies the Museum's P-47 before restoration for a familiarisation flight (Bill Painter). **Below:** Air Zoo A&P Dick Schaus examines the firewall during initial stages of the disassembly. **Lower:** Col. Gabreski raised his score to 37 1/2 victories in Korea to become a double Ace; seen here alongside the Air Zoo's P-47D in 1991.*

Kalamazoo Thunderbolt

not suffered because of the modification and full power is still available for take off. It is only at high altitude, where the turbo is in demand that performance diminishes and the *Air Zoo's* P-47 typically does not fly that high.

It also seems likely that the aircraft was in an accident during which the right wing was damaged beyond repair as there was evidence that the wing which it now has, originally had a speed brake. Sheet metal work was needed to fair in the areas where the brake doors had been and to take care of corrosion on the ventral surface of the wing. But actually the P-47 was in pretty good shape. Especially considering it was an Air Force airframe which generally would not have as much corrosion proofing as a Naval aircraft.

Because of the elements (salt water) to which a Navy plane is subjected, preventative measures such as cadmium plating and anodising have been built to protect it. Though an air force airframe would have some of these preventative measures, they would not be as extensive as in a machine that was going to be exposed to the corrosive sea air. Also, though the plane spent most of it's life in what one would think was the jungle heat and humidity of Peru, in reality much of the country is very dry.

Other problems that surfaced were the old military gyros which tended to tumble during aerobatics, and vacuum pump failures - three of them! The gyros were easily replaced but the restoration team had a heck of a time finding out what the problem was with the pump. Finally, after very close inspection, Bob Ellis discovered that a base plate on the engine was installed incorrectly at the factory, blocking one of the oil passages that fed the system. This reduced the oil circulation sufficiently so that the vacuum pump would overheat and burn up in about 10 hours.

The hydraulics were another problem. Technology of the late 30's and early 40's simply was not compatible with the technology of today. Consequently, seals for the hydraulic cylinders and landing gear were not available. The problem was solved by redesigning the sealing surfaces to be suitable with modern seals. Bearings were no problem, *Kal-Aero Inc.* did the avionics, and the museum team installed the airframe wiring.

Since the aircraft had never been in World War II combat, the museum did not feel compelled to paint it in a scheme historically accurate to 49181. Various paint designs were considered with the idea of finding one which was dramatic and had nationwide appeal. When received, the aircraft sported the green nose found on the aircraft in Les Friends 149th Fighter Squadron. The *Air Zoo* initially changed it to a red cowling, rudder and lateral fuselage stripe similar to the 527th Fighter Squadron (which did not have the red rudder). Matt black anti-glare panels and post WW II Bars and Stars completed the

scheme. Historically, there was a Thunderbolt called *Gal* from Kalamazoo, and this paint scheme was considered when it came time to repaint, but it was dismissed as not having wide enough appeal. Finally the scheme of Col.Francis Gabreski's ship was chosen since he had been the top American ace in Europe, a facsimile of his plane would be immediately recognisable. After almost three years and 10,000 man hours, the big bird was ready to reclaim the sky in June 1984.

The first test flight of the newly restored Thunderbolt was a little more exciting than most. Over the years, museum pilots had flown the first flights of the newly restored Corsair, Stearman, Warhawk and Hellcat. All of these flights had been uneventful and there was no reason to believe that this one would be any different. Perhaps this is the reason why this test was flown after hours and museum pilot Pete Parish simply flew the Thunderbolt off into the wild blue yonder. Typically, such a first flight would consist of circling the field several times, but Bob Ellis and Bill Painter found themselves standing there watching as the P-47 turned into a little dot and disappeared. Half an hour later, Bob began to worry - considerably! Finally the drone of the 2800 was heard and the plane reappeared, but there was a problem.

The aircraft is on final and looking good. All of a sudden power comes on, gear up and the heavy bird climbs for the sky. Pete approached again, flaps down, gear down. Again he pulled out of it, making another circuit. Via the tower, Bob discovered that the landing gear, though down, was not registering as being locked, and Pete really did not want to have a failure causing this newly restored craft to belly in. Pete had tried several manoeuvres suggested by the manual to snap the gear in place and reported 1200lbs of hydraulic pressure....the crash crew

was notified that there was a problem and to be ready for a potential accident. Bob told Pete to land.

Gently the ship settled towards the earth. Pete slowly cut back on the power and yawed the '47 ever so slightly, the tyres skimming the strip. Finally, he eased the massive plane down, full weight coming onto the gear - it held. As soon as the P-47 taxied in Bob inspected the gear to find that the left down lock pin was not in place because the gear was extending slightly beyond the correct position. Simple shimming took care of the problem.

Competition at the *Experimental Aircraft Association Convention* Oshkosh was tough in 1984 with the Thunderbolt being awarded EAA *Judges Choice*. Jack Levine and Bill Pryors magnificent F9F Panther earned the *Grand Champion* while Jack Rose's P-51 *Worry Bird* took Reserve. The *Jug* is a beautiful ship though, and one of only six that still ply the skies.

You can see this Thunderbolt along with such classics as the P-51 Mustang, P-40 Warhawk, B-25 Mitchell, P-39 Airacobra, FG-1D Corsair, HA-1112 Buchon, the Grumman Cats (Wildcat, Hellcat, Tigercat and Bearcat), along with a variety of other warbirds at the *Kalamazoo Air Zoo*. And you can visit by either car or plane. By car, take the I-94 to the Portage Rd. exit (78). Take Portage Rd. South two traffic lights. At Milham Rd. turn left (east) and the museum is at the end of the road. By plane, simply fly to the *Kalamazoo/Battle Creek International Airport* and taxi up on the museum's flight deck. For more information write: The *Kalamazoo Aviation History Museum*, 3101 East Milham Rd., Kalamazoo, MI 49002-1700, or call (616) 382-6555.WW *Gerard Pahl, Kalamazoo Aviation History Museum.*

Information provided by: Francis Gabreski, Ed Jurist, Rick Cahow, Tim Savage, Bob Ellis, Dick Schaus, Ted Damick and Bill Painter.

The Kalamazoo Air Zoo's P-47 Thunderbolt over Michigan Woodlands. (Philip Makanna of GHOSTS Photo).

WARBIRDS AIRNEWS

AUSTRALIA

The **DH.82A Tiger Moth VH-SGH** of the **R.A.A.F. Museum** crashed on December 1 1991 killing the instructor Group Captain Michael Birks, the pupil Flight Lieutenant Richard Davies being injured. The accident happened when the aircraft was coming in to land at R.A.A.F. Point Cook.

One of only two remaining **CAC Mk 23 Mustangs** extant, **A68-137/VH-PPV** is nearing completion following retraction tests at Townsville In Queensland. The aircraft is painted in distinctive 3 Squadron grey/green camouflage with distinctive blue and white Southern Cross rudder. Report by David Daly.

GREAT BRITAIN

The **Fighter Collection** continues to move their aircraft onto the U.K.register; Corsair FG1-D has become G-FGID, their **Bristol Fighter,** under restoration with *Skysport* at Hatch, Bedfordshire, has been re-allocated its former-registration G-ACAA, while the ex **Swedish A.F. Harvard** has been registered G-BTXI. Coming in as Tempest II PR536 was going out was the new Yakovlev Yak-50, which was given the in-sequence registration G-BTZB. The centre section and fuselage frame have been completed by The Aircraft Restoration Company. The **Sea Fury VX653,** exchanged for the Tempest II has also arrived at Duxford. It had apparently gone straight into the R.A.F. Museum from store, arriving at Duxford with guns and an exposed film in the camera gun!

The 'Collections low back Mk.XIV Spitfire **G-SPIT (MV293)** has had it's engine mounted, and it is planned to paint this aircraft in a basic silver scheme. At **Chino** the **Lockheed P-38 Lightning** was well into it's flight test programme, some ten hours of flying being completed with *Fighter Rebuilders* as this edition went to press. Arriving just before Christmas was an **AD-4N Skyraider F-AZED,** bought

from the *Amicale Jean Baptiste Salis* at La Ferté Alais. It arrived at it's new Duxford home on Christmas Eve, the pilot being T.F.C.Director Hoof Proudfoot. The Collection has also added ex **Charles Church Spitfire's Limited Mk. XIV SM832** to its ranks. **Bristol Blenheim 10210 of The Aeroplane Restoration Company** has had the tail section mated to the airframe and is now standing on it's own undercarriage - there will be a major feature on this in the next edition.

At **North Weald** Dave Gilmour has formalised his collection of aircraft by creating the **Intrepid Aviation Company.** It now consists of Stampe G-BKBK, Stearman N4596N, Staggerwing G-BRVE, his rare SNJ-7, Mustang 44-74008, and Gnat G-MOUR. They are all based at North Weald.

Hispano HA-1112 Mil Buchon G-HUNN (once of the *Charles Church collection*) has been struck off the U.K.register and has been sold to *Sherman Aircraft* in the U.S.A. Also heading for the USA in January was the collection's CCF **Hurricane G-ORGI,** which has been sold to **The Museum of Flying**

Though the **Old Flying Machine Company** has a reputation for going a long way to attend a display, New Zealand must be something of a first! The O.F.M.C. Hispano 'Me109J' G-BOML is due to display at the **Warbirds Over Wanaka** show that takes place over the Easter weekend. The aircraft will be shipped over and air freighted back in time for the U.K. air display season. Looking new in it's primer paint is the O.F.M.C. **Spitfire Mk.XIV MV730 G-FXIV.** This restoration is to static condition.

The shuffling at the **R.A.F. Museum** Hendon continues, the composite **Bristol Beaufort** is now installed alongside the Bristol Beaufighter forming part of Coastal Command display. The Beaufort was acquired from David Tallichet, and after the main restoration was completed at R.A.F. Cardington, the fabric work was undertaken by *Historic Flying*. Out goes the previous incumbent, the Spanish Dornier Do.24 that has been sent on indefinite loan to the Netherlands, while the new **P-51D** joins the other aircraft in the Bomber Command Hall. Going overseas to **Norway** is the **Mosquito**.

At **Autokraft,** they have run the engine installed in **Hawker Hurricane Mk.XII G-HURR** at Brooklands on October 25th. This looks like being the first of *Autokraft's* various Hawker types to fly, the big event probably being sometime this spring.

Spitfire Tr 9 PV 202/G-TRIX has been sold by Robert Parker to Rick Roberts. It was rebuilt by Steve Atkins.

The U.K. scene has managed to retain what had been it's first pure warbird show that until recently

From David Daly comes this excellent photograph of VH-PPV alias A68-137. The aircraft has been a long term rebuild project in Townsville, Queensland, Australia but is now nearing completion.

looked doomed. With the closure of **West Malling** in Kent, the **Great Warbirds Airshow** seemed likely to fold due to the lack of a base. However, arrangements have been made with **Wroughton,** Wiltshire, home of the *Science Museum's* reserve collection and a Fleet Air Arm storage centre to hold the show there. The date is August 30/31, and it will be the 11th *Great Warbirds Airshow.*

Seen at Wroughton last year was the **British Aerospace's Mosquito RR299,** which is about to undergo a major overhaul, including a complete strip of the fabric from the plywood covered frame. This will hopefully see the aircraft take on new colours, those it has borne for many years now being from the film *Mosquito Squadron*. Audley End based *Historic Flying* have secured the contract to refabric the aircraft and the project is being overseen by Director Clive Denney.

Gloster Meteor F.8 VZ467 has been registered G-METE and is under restoration at Cosford, being registered to *Air Support Aviation Services* of London. In 1974 when on the charge of 229 O.C.U. at Brawdy VZ467 was painted in the colours of 615 Squadron and christened *Winston* in commemo-

Underside view of The Alpine Fighter Collection's Birdcage Corsair shows the RNZAF camouflage pattern to advantage. Formerly with Harry Dona and later Roy Stafford and the late Don Knapp, Tim Wallis purchased the Corsair in the USA in 1991 - it will be one of the stars at the forthcoming show detailed below. (**Norman Pealing**)

have been mated to the fuselage and engineer Ray Mulqueen is working flat out to see the aircraft in the air by the end of March.

WARBIRDS OVER WANAKA

The **Warbirds over Wanaka Airshow** is shaping up again to be the major attraction of the New Zealand airshow season. Wanaka nestles amongst the mountains and lakes and provides an ideal setting for this action packed event and plans are well advanced with many major attractions now confirmed, including the resident F4U-1 and P-40K.

The most exciting will be a visit from the UK of a 'Bf109J' flown by former New Zealander **Ray Hanna**. **Mark Hanna** will fly the *Alpine Fighter Collection's* Spitfire featured in *Warbirds Worldwide Number 12*. Negotiations are currently under way for the visit of Lockheed duo in the form of a **Lodestar** and **Neptune**. And of course the world renowned **Roaring Forties** aerobatic team which has recently performed in the United States and Australia. To help sponsor the Messerschmitt's visit from England a number of Gold Passes

Continued on Page 14

ration of Winston Churchill who was an honourary Air Commodore of 615 Sqn. (a companion Meatbox being christened *Clementine*). The aircraft was last flown on October 22nd 1982, and has since been in storage at various R.A.F. stations. At last the U.K. has a North American F86A registered and available for airshow work. Reported in the last issue, the **F-86A** has now been registered G-SABR to Golden Apple Operations. (See feature on page 25).

It is our sad duty to report the death of **John 'Jeff' Hawke.** He was an extrovert who will be remembered for his exuberant displays and film flying in several types. For many, his display performances in the B-25 Mitchell during the late seventies and early eighties epitomise the image that Hawke created. The circumstances in which he died are still somewhat sketchy, his body being found still strapped into the cockpit of a Piper Aztec that had crashed into the Adriatic off the coast of Chiogga.

Arthur Gibson, the renowned aviation photographer died soon after a heart attack recently. Well known for his outstanding still and motion photography Arthur was a former R.A.F. and volunteer Reserve pilot. He and his specially

The Fighter Collection's Sea Fury awaits delivery outside the RAF Museum at Hendon. The aircraft is 100% stock, apparently having been placed into storage following retirement from the Royal Navy. It is now at Duxford awaiting rebuild. (James Kightly)

modified camera ship (appropriately registered G-FOTO) had become a familiar sight at many displays throughout the U.K. In 1984 he and a band of display pilots organised the first **Fighter Meet** at North Weald in Essex and earned high acclaim for his subsequently annual warbird airshow. Gibson was also part owner of **Plane Sailing's** Consolidated PBY-5A Catalina G-BLSC and F7F Tigercat N6178C. He will be greatly missed by both pilots, friends and enthusiasts alike who have been deprived of the innovative quality of his photographic work.

NEW ZEALAND

The **Alpine Fighter Collection's F4U-1A Birdcage Corsair** Bu17995 (ex N90285) has been imported in to New Zealand and registered as ZK-FUI. It is now painted as NZ5201, the first Corsair serving with the Royal New Zealand Air Force and the aircraft has seen extensive flying since it arrived. The colour shot opposite shows *Warbirds Worldwide* member Keith Skilling at the controls **(Norman Pealing photograph)**. Also at **Wanaka** the same organisation's **P-40K** 42-9733 is progressing very well. The wings

WARBIRDS AIRNEWS

will be made available at $100 NZ dollars per ticket. Further information is available from *Warbirds Over Wanaka*, P.O. Box 218, Wanaka. Preparations are being made for a crowd of 30-40,000 in this superb setting. At the last show Tim Wallis even managed to organise a superb display of the Southern Lights!

THAILAND

At Chieng Mei R.T.A.F. Air Base, the R.T.A.F. is restoring a **Spitfire** to airworthy condition. Available are an anonymous **Mk.XIV** given the Thai code U14/1/93 and a **PR.XIX** U14/30/93, ex PS 836 in R.A.F. service. Target date for the first flight is August 1992, the Queen of Thailand's 60th birthday.

ITALY

An authentic example of one of Italy's most historic fighters, the Macchi **MC200** Saetta(Lightning) has recently been restored for the **USAF Museum** at Dayton, Ohio by the company that was responsible for its design, development and manufacture. The company (Aermacchi) is still located at Varese in Northern Italy where the MC200 programme was centred. A remarkably advanced project for the mid-1930s, the MC200 is a retractable gear, radial engined monoplane, and was the first single seat fighter to be designed by Macchi's brilliant technical manager, Dr. Ing. Mario Castoldi of Schneider racing fame (the designation MC being an abbreviation for Macchi-Castoldi) Powered by a 850hp Fiat engine, the prototype made its first flight on December 24th 1937 with test pilot Giuseppe Burei at the controls. A total of 156 MC200s were in service with the Regia Aeronautica when the nation entered the war in June 1940 and the type was employed over Malta (where it made its operational debut) and Yugoslavia, Greece, North Africa, the Soviet Union and in the defence of Italy.

This particular example of the MC200 series was captured by Allied Forces in November 1942 in the course of the Battle of El Alamein. It had to be abandoned at Benghazi's K3 airfield during the Axis retreat.

In the subsequent sharing of the spoils of war the MC200 was shipped to the United States

The MC-200 Saetta during restoration at the Aermacchi facility at Varese. One leading UK collector, having seen the work has stated the aircraft could fly. It is destined for the USAF Museum at Dayton (M. Longoni)

along with a Ju87 and an Me109. All three were exhibited in the USA to raise war bond funds. The MC200 was coded 372-5 indicating it was originally assigned to the 372nd Squadriglia. This unit was based in Italy but is known to have passed on some of its aircraft to units operating in North Africa. n this instance the aircraft was lost only three days after arrival at its new unit, the 165th Squadriglia.

Due to a lack of interest in the aircraft immediately after the war it was simply placed in a childrens playground. However, in the 1960s it was purchased by the Bradley Air Museum (now the New England Air Museum) in Conneticut. The museum lacked the manpower and financial resources to undertake the restoration but all possible steps were taken to prevent further deterioration.

In 1989 the aircraft was purchased from the museum by a private owner, with the aim of having it completely restored by Aermacchi, prior to donating it to the USAF Museum. The aircraft arrived at Varese in December 1989. The task of restoration was indeed formidable. the corrosion that had occurred while this fine old fighter had stood 20 years in the rian had virtually destroyed half of the airframe, including the cowling, the horizontal tail, the canopy structure and many internal fittings. Some important items were missing including the three blade propeller..

Despite seemingly insurmountable problems the MC200 is now fully restored to exhibition standard although there is no intention to make the fighter airworthy (Editor's note: one leading UK collector, upon inspecting the work has stated the quality is unbelievable and the aircraft could be made to fly). The effort has taken almost two years and has involved thousands of man hours by a team of highly skilled Aermacchi workers. Using the original drawings, hundreds of detail parts have been manufactured from scratch, using Mil-standard quality materials and processes. The complex structure of the wings has been stripped bare, repaired and completely reskinned. The undercarriage and the powerplant have been disassembled and renovated with loving care by experts who are intent on maintaining the company's tradition of excellence,

Credit is also due to members of G.A.V.S. (the Italian Historical Aircraft Group) for researching the history of this particular MC20, preparing a detailed colour study and locating a number of essential items. These include the aircraft's instruments, the tail wheel, the main undercarriage wheels and tyres, the pitot tubes and many other important elements.

Today, almost 50 years since its construction, this MC200 Saetta is ready to cross the Atlantic for a third time. On this occasion it will be carried in a strategic transport

aircraft of Military Airlift Command to join other exhibits in the USAF Museum at Dayton, Ohio. The MC200 will be the only Italian aircraft in the Dayton Collection, although there is a second Macchi fighter (an MC202) at the National Air and Space Museum in Washington, D.C. Together, these historic fighters serve as a permanent reminder of the Regia Aeronautica's widespread but little known operations during World War II.

The Editor would like to thank Maurizio Longoni for the story and photographs on this remarkable project.

UNITED STATES

Exciting news from the United States includes information on an exciting new project being undertaken by John MacGuire's War Eagles Air Museum located in New Mexico. The museum imported an ex Chinese TU-2 bomber last year and the aircraft will be rebuilt to flying condition. This is just one of several new projects being undertaken by the museum.

The Weeks Air Museum have acquired an A-20G (c/n 21844), N34290. Operated by the Hughes Aircraft Company of Culver City, California from 1963 until 1972 when ownership passed to the Antelope Valley Aero Museum at Lancaster, California. The aircraft was moved to Fox Field in the same state, though the proposed new Milestones of Flight Museum floundered. The aircraft will be moved to Florida and put into storage to await its turn for restoration.

Thierry Thomassin's last visit to Chino provided us with some superb photographs of activities at the **Yankee Air Corps Museum** where Stan Hoeffler continues to work magic on the collection.

On the P-40 front, **P-40E N9837A,** (ex AK899, c/n 15370) is nearing completion. Owned by Warbirds Worldwide member Richard Hansen of Batavia, Illinois the aircraft ran its JRS *Enterprises* rebuilt Allison engine for the first time on October 24th 1991. It has been rebuilt by a subsidiary of *Blackhawk Airways* of Janesville, Wisconsin

YANKEE AIR CORPS

*These photographs were all taken by Thierry Thomassin at Chino late in 1991 and show progress at **The Yankee Air Corps** on numerous projects: **Large Pictures - Top** - The Yankee Air Corp's second FM2 Wildcat, Bu86819, N5833 which was (in the late 1950's used for crop dusting). The other Wildcat is Bu86564, N4629V which was formerly with Tallmantz Aviation/Movieland of The Air. **Bottom:** Now on its main gear, RP-63C Kingcobra 43-11117 which was formerly a gate guard at Hammer AFB, California. **Small pictures clockwise:** Still on the Bell theme is P-39 the fuselage of which is making rapid progress. P-47M Ex Bendix racer NX4477N once owned by Bill Odom and raced in the famous 1942 Bendix event is now registered N4477M. Actually a YP-47M, serial 42-27385 it was obtained from the now famous Victory Air Museum at Mundellin in Illinois. P-63A Kingcobra N94501 is serial 42-65080 and is painted and on permanent display in the museum facility. A long term restoration and a rare one into the bargain is P-51A 43-6274 (c/n 99-22377).*

RUSSIAN THUNDER

Rock Star **Gary Numan** explains his deep and meaningful relationship with Eddie Coventry's Yak 11. **John Dibbs** took the pictures.

Over the years I've longed to own many different types of aeroplane. A good measure of how deep the longing has been can be measured by my small plastic model aircraft collection. One Skyraider, one Hurricane, one Zero, two Sea Furies, three Spitfires, three Mustangs, three Harvards and four Corsairs at the last count. The more models I make of each type, the more my desire for the real thing. If I could find a decent model kit of the Yak 11 I think I would buy five, putting it high on my list of aeroplanes to dream about.

Luckily, I have been able to buy, and operate for many years now, my own Harvard, and, through owning it, I've become deeply involved in display flying. In 1985 I joined the *Harvard Formation Team* and came to know Anthony Hutton, the team's founder and leader, quite well. It was Anthony who first told me about the Yak 11. He had owned one of the very first machines to come to the west, flying it at many displays and eventually selling it in the USA. He had nothing but praise for this Russian marvel, which, until then, I had barely even heard of. His stories of the Yaks' remarkably high performance for just a fraction of the operating cost of the big and powerful World War II fighters, fired in me an interest in the type that has grown increasingly over the past few years as I've slowly found out more about this incredible aircraft. Some of the stories that I was told seemed *too* amazing to believe. I couldn't understand why, if it was so good, more people didn't rave about the machine. Anthony had often said, that for your hard earned pound (or Dollar), the Yak 11 gave more units of pleasure than any other machine of it's kind. Thanks to the kindness of one man I was to find out some years later that it was every bit as impressive as I had been led to believe, perhaps even more so.

My first real encounter with the Yak 11 happened about two years ago at North Weald when I was allowed to sit in the aeroplane then owned by well known British collector Robs Lamplough. Standing silently on the taxiway I remember being very impressed by it's squat and powerful looks. The wide track undercarriage and what seemed to me at the time incredibly short wings only added to it's almost menacing appearance. As I slid down into the front seat I was surprised at how small the cockpit seemed compared to the cavernous expanse of my Harvard. The Yak 11, unlike the Harvard, has a floor of sorts and a much lower canopy that gave me, for a moment, a slightly claustrophobic feeling, although this soon passed. However, it did make me feel more a part of the aeroplane rather than something that I was just strapping myself into. I've heard other pilots referring to it as 'wearing the aeroplane'.

First flown in 1946, the Yak 11 is a direct descendant of the famous and highly successful family of Yak fighters of the second World War. It's wing and basic construction owing much to it's potent ancestors. The two seat tandem cockpit is similar in basic style to the better known and more plentiful North American T-6 although quite different in detail. It was originally designed as an advanced combat trainer and, including 707 machines built in Czechoslovakia as the C-11, some 4,557 were manufactured.

Climbing out of the cockpit of Robs' aeroplane I was left with the overwhelming impression that the Yak was something of a hot ship and I must confess to being more than a little intimidated by it. A problem of having most your hours on one particular type, in my case the Harvard, is that you tend to use that type as a yardstick by which to measure others. I suppose it's unavoidable in some ways but it led me to form, on that brief initial meeting, an entirely incorrect opinion of the Yak 11.

In August 1991 I was spending an afternoon with Eddie Coventry, a well known air racing pilot in the U.K. Eddie had been having some difficulty landing his Yak-11 (G-OYAK), and so fellow Radial Pair team member Norman Lees and myself had been helping to sort out the problem. Firstly, by Eddie flying with me in my Harvard and then, shortly after, by him flying in the Yak with Norman who had flown Robs Lamplough's aeroplane previously and so had some useful experience on the type. I later discovered that the Yak is a lot easier to land than the Harvard so I doubt that I did Eddie any favours at all.

After Eddie had completed a solo detail that same afternoon, his landing problem very quickly becoming a thing of the past, he kindly offered Norman and myself the opportunity to fly his aeroplane. Personally I couldn't wait. The BAC Windows sponsored Yak is a Czech built example and had in it's past been operated by the Egyptian Air Force; it was one of 40 recovered from there by Jean Salis. I had watched this aeroplane undergo a painstaking rebuild for the last four years in the very capable hands of Phil Parrish and his team at Earls Colne, a small airfield in the south of England. It was beautifully prepared and a great credit to all those involved. As I slid down into the front seat of a Yak 11 for the second time in my life the sense of responsibility was clutching at my heart.

This was the first time that anybody had entrusted their much loved, high performance warbird into my care. I had been flying my Harvard at air shows for over seven years and had for a long time dreamed of moving up the horse power ladder, waiting patiently for the offer that I had hoped would one day be made. I was extremely grateful to Eddie, very excited and keen to get airborne. I'd read and reread the short but highly informative pilots notes compiled many years previously by Neil Williams and soon found myself making some sense of the many knobs, levers, valves and buttons in the cockpit, thankfully feeling none of the claustrophobia that I'd felt at North Weald in Robs' machine. Norman, standing on the left of the wing, gave me a very thorough briefing on the systems and the sorts of things I could expect. I had already written down on

my trusty knee board all the speeds and power settings that I would need, plus some that I desperately hope that I would not. After carefully reading the pre-start check list it was time to fire up the machine.

The Yak 11 is essentially a pneumatic aeroplane. The brakes, flaps, undercarriage and even the engine starter are all operated from air pressure stored, in Eddie's Yak, in two air bottles in the fuselage. They hold the main auxiliary supplies. There is also a third emergency bottle. All three bottles are kept up to pressure by an on board air compressor that operates whenever the engine is running.

Powered by an 820 horse power Shvetsov seven cylinder radial engine, the Yak is in the British system of air display grouping a group C aeroplane. This group is for any single piston engined aircraft over 600 horse power and below 5700kg.

Starting the Shvetsov, like so many aero engines of it's era, is definitely a pass-time more suited to an octopus than a human being although, up to a point, it is fairly straightforward.

Check that the undercarriage lever is selected down, main or auxiliary air valve open, master switch on, check two greens, fuel switch on, flap lever neutral, throttle 1/4 inch open, pitch lever to max rpm, fuel cock open, idle cut off to run,

magnetos on, oil cooler closed, gills closed, pump up the fuel pressure with the slightly awkwardly placed wobble pump, prime the engine, up to 10 strokes on a coldish day and then it starts to get a tad tricky. The Yak 11 has no parking brake and, as your hands are more than occupied with other things, you cannot hold the aeroplane manually on the brakes by gripping the hand operated lever on the stick. It helps to have at least one ground crew person available so that you can start the aeroplane against some chocks.

Hold the stick back between your knees, press the booster coil button on the upper left hand side of the main instrument panel with your left hand, whilst opening the start valve on the outside of the right console with your right hand. Any extra priming, wobbling or throttle tweaking is made in a series of frantic grabs around the cockpit. Actually, most of the time, the Schvetsov starts very well. Starting the engine uses air at an incredible rate and the start valve must be closed the second that the engine fires. If the motor is bit reluctant to start do not keep the valve open in an effort to keep the engine turning as the air pressure will be gone in 10-25 seconds at the most and that will be that: no air, no starter. Using an external air bottle to supply the air for starting is a good idea particularly when the internal air pressures are low.

Some Yak owners fit small electric compressors in their aeroplanes so that, by connecting a suitable ground power unit, the internal air bottles can be topped up without having to start the engine. This seems to be an excellent arrangement, taking away much of the worry of operating the aeroplane away from home and I believe Eddie intends to fit such a system to G-OYAK.

Once the engine is running smoothly it should be warmed between 1000 and 1200 rpm. The oil is very slow to warm up and you should allow a minimum of fifteen minutes between your start up and take off times on anything but a very warm day. My first start went very well. The engine came to life immediately in a very

Continued on Page 22

Wing to Wing

Dave Clinton of **Darton International** outlines the basics of formation flying and details the forthcoming release of a new training film on the subject.

Top: View of a perfect right echelon from the lead aircraft. Shown is Dan Lawson, Dave Clinton and Les Salz. Below: In position! Both photographs courtesy Dave Clinton.

Throughout the recorded history of mankind, we can very precisely trace most of our actions and aspirations and indeed our survival by imitating other creatures in nature. In pre-historic times, the wild food we ate from vegetation was the result of observing other mammals eating.

So it is in aviation. We aspired to have a different perspective of the planet, or a bird's eye view. Man, never being content, continued to forge ahead ever emulating the actions of birds, our winged friends. Our first aviation history records this emulation of flight because it was something new and challenging. In formation flight, it soon became evident the real value of such flight was not necessarily the visual beauty it formed, but the mutual protection of the elements within the flight.

Nothing is as majestic or breath taking as a full flight of Canadian Snow Geese or North American Mallards. Even field sparrows sometimes engage in such precise formation flight with so many participants that you question what form of communication allows such precision. Many basics of formation flight that took man years to learn ie: the geometry and fluid positions required to conserve energy, are natural to the birds.

Formation flight as we know it today has it's roots in military aviation. Obviously, the purpose is perfectly clear - there is safety in numbers. For strategic and tactical considerations, especially considering bomber group activity, World War II statistics proved that large formations provided the only effective way to reach targets with any certainty of delivering massive amounts of ordnance. The formation doctrine continues to undergo evolutionary change as the result of available weapons systems. Because the term formation implies more than one, it is acknowledged that the foundation of any formation flight is a two ship. Two ships, four ships, six ships, etc. are all based on the premise of a leader and a wingman. Again, based on military doctrine, the position of the wingman in relation to the leader, or a second pair and their respective position, is dictated by the tactics and the mission to be undertaken. For fighters, when departing home base in route to the target area and then returning, they might undergo many formation changes during the flight depending on considerations

such as weather, fuel supply, ordnance delivery, in-route flight, and recovery at home base.

Tactically speaking, a division, or two sections, which is a leader and his wingman and a section leader and his wingman, might in separate section take-offs, climb in parade formation and transition to in-route cruise for air-to-air refuelling and then assume a combat spread for ordnance delivery.

All formation flight requires long and arduous hours of practice, practice, *practice*. In the military, your formation flight training began immediately after the completion of basic flight training. No longer would you look on a military flying career based on a solo condition, but as one of a group.

The principles of formation flying are rooted in basic aerodynamics with the applications and understanding of geometry. The most important factor involved in formation flying is the RECOGNITION AND CONTROL OF RELA-

TIVE MOTION. The precise techniques used to control relative motion deal with the physics of flight and geometry. In all our flying careers, the basis of aircraft control certainly has been the control of relative motion, but with parameters much larger than would be tolerated in precise formation flight. In the most stringent test standards, you would only be required to maintain altitude at + or - 50 feet, and sometimes this seems very difficult. In formation flight, you are required to maintain parameters of + or - 1 or 2 feet, relatively speaking, while making corrections so smooth as to be imperceptible. The criteria is very simple in formation flying - you are either in formation or out of formation - there is no between.

In formation, the core manoeuvre is what is called station keeping. In the flight condition of station keeping for two aircraft, the wingman is required to maintain precise relative distance from the leader in three planes. One: wingtip.

Two: height. Three: longitudinal, or nose to tail. Each military organisation may specify the exact distances for each one of these planes and this may be peculiar to the type of aeroplane. In my training background in the U.S. Navy, proper position was wingtip clearance to nose-to-tail clearance, and enough step-down clearance to allow free, uninterrupted or unobstructed movement by the leader. This does not necessarily hold true depending on the flight or tactical situation. In the 1940s and 1950s. it was appropriate to configure formations stepped-up to facilitate a type of ordnance delivery or tactical intercept.

In all U.S Military organisations today, for fixed-wing aircraft a proper formation will be stepped-down. Safety dictates that wingtip clearance be maintained and stepped down be maintained even though there may be nose to tail overlap. From this station keeping, parade formation, aircraft may disperse to combat spreads that are line abreast, echelon or in trail.

For the wingman to maintain a precise position in station-keeping, all controls of the aircraft are used, ie: primary flight controls and power controls. Station-keeping in the parade position is not in smooth air. The disturbed air bubble surrounding the leader significantly increases the workload necessary to maintain precise station-keeping. Sometimes measurable changes are needed in trim depending on which side of lead you are on - left or right. This is one principle we must accept in formation flying in spite of the fact we cannot see it. However, we must constantly be cautious and aware of these unseen forces because they result in aircraft movement that may not necessarily be commanded by input. Sometimes the best formation pilots can maintain station in smooth air with such imperceptible changes in control movements as to defy their use. This then, is the essence of the task: concentration to the exclusion of all other mental inputs except the task at hand - maintaining position.

The skill required to do this are learned. I suppose every pilot is potentially capable of learning to fly formation, but my personal experience is that like in every other human task, some people are better than others.

The geometry and physics of formation flight change depending on the flight plane we are engaged in. Level turns, with no acceleration change except of dynamics, result in difference radius' of turn that we require a wingman to change power if he wishes to maintain position. Obviously, on the outside of the turn the wingman is flying a larger arc than the leader and will need more power. Conversely, on the inside of the turn the opposite is true. To maintain precise position, the wingman must instantly recognise that change in relative motion and provide the proper control input.

The description of a fingertip is where the wingman rotates around the axis of the leader in the turn. If you are on the right wing and the leader enters a left turn, to maintain finger tip position, you will need to add power, climb, and a turn at a greater rate than the leader while equalling his relative angle of bank. All this must be recognized and instantly accommodated at the time the turn is begun or completed. In an echelon turn, the wingman rotates about his own axis while still in a larger arc than the leader. The term echelon and fingertip describe relative position of the wingman in a turn.

In free-cruise formations, the formation is further spread and the wingman uses the geometry of flight by either turning or outside the leaders turn to maintain relative nose-to-tail position. Introducing vertical components to manouvering whether in parade or free cruise formation introduces the dynamics of acceleration and deceleration. Of course, arcs and radials are no longer strictly dependant upon horizontal components, but are a combination of horizontal and vertical components. As a training manoeuvre, all military aviators will engage in lazy eights, or in the military, as wingovers, which go through 90 degree angles of bank and back-to-back 180 degree turns.

These types of manoeuvres begin to prepare aviators for tactical manoeuvres used in air combat. Each military branch has it's own particular doctrine regarding types of positions but they all have to do with the goal of prevailing in flight. Typically, the wingman is relegated to the position of protectorate for the leader, though not always. For instance, the air force uses a 'double attack doctrine, while the navy uses a 'loose deuce'. We won't go into the detail with the pluses and minuses, but each allows the wingman to act offensively or defensively while allowing t precisely maintain his position in a formed formation.

In the U.S. the civilian warbird community is well developed with many types of aircraft routinely flown by civilian pilots, many of whom have never had formal formation training. Most of the organisations in the U.S. that sponsor or

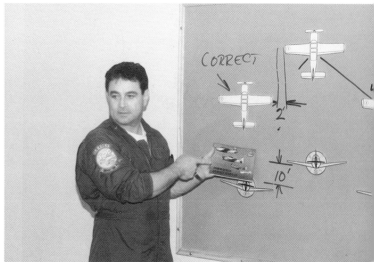

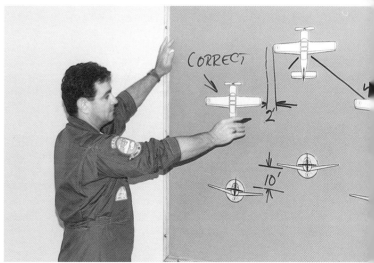

Page 18 Top: Returning from a formation flying film sortie.Bottom: Perfect wing on a formation take-off. This Page: Top: dave Clinton in the classroom showing proper wing tip spacing during a Darton International Ground School. Above: Proper position on a three-ship formation take off. Lead - John Harrison, left wing Dave Clinton, Right Wing: Dan Lawson. Dave Clinton is heavily involved with the T-28 both through his company - which offers a large range of T-28 related products and services and through The North American Trainer Association (NATA). NATA membership is open to all at the exceptional membership rate of $40.00 (U.S. and Canada or $50.00 elsewhere - U.S. Funds or IMO or now by Visa/Mastercard, Contact Kathy Stonich at NATA 25801 N.E. Hinness Rd., Brush Prarie, WA 98606, U.S.A. Tel: (206) 256 0066 or Fax 206 896 5398

support demonstration flying at airshows have their requirements for allowing individuals or groups to engage in formation flight. The organisations I am familiar with, *Warbirds of America*, and the *North American Trainer Association*, have adopted the Formation Flight Manual developed by the T-34 *Association*. The principles, procedures and language of formation flight is contained in this concise booklet. It is a compilation of U.S.Navy and U.S. Air Force doctrine that has been filtered and best fits the civilian environment.

As of this writing, many U.S. organisations will not allow individuals to fly in airshows sponsored by them unless they have been 'patched'. In effect, this is an oral exam and a flight test as described in the T-34 manual with levels of performance graded satisfactory or unsatisfactory. The procedure does not attempt to grade based on the criteria of the *Blue Angels* or *Thunderbirds*, but of competence and safety. The flight check requires two similar aircraft and two authorised check pilots. The check pilots are designated by the respective organisation.

Formation flying is not for everyone. You can certainly enjoy a warbird and the airshow circuit without engaging in formation flight. Some people just don't enjoy the level of concentration necessary to enjoy safe, precise formation flight. But for those who do and are not military trained, flight training curriculums are rare. In addition, the process is long, expensive and arduous. As the result of my personal involve-

ment in the warbird community, I am continually requested to provide formation training. Seizing upon the opportunity our firm, *Darton International*, embarked upon a course to produce a professional program called *The Art of Formation Flying*. This hour long film, shot mostly from the perspective of the wingman, deals with the basics, the physics, and the dynamics of formation flight using the military doctrine. The film will be narrated, set to music, and will contain classroom presentations necessary for the beginner to understand the concepts of formation flight. I believe it is a very entertaining film in addition to the training provided.

While no one hour film could replace the months of formation training available in the military, the film goes a long way towards providing a pictorial situational awareness of what formation flight looks like when it is right and wrong and what the corrections should be. The film will be available by the Spring of 1992 in all international video formats. Look out for announcements in *Warbirds Worldwide*.

For those of you who are qualified pilots, the word is always the same: *currency* and *safety*. For those who aspire to become formation pilots, the words dedication, training and concentration should have the utmost meaning because they represent the necessary investment to become a good formation pilot. WW Dave Clinton

LOOKING FOR A T-28?

A small ad in *Trade-A-Plane* recently caught my eye. I had seen it before but had not thought much about it. It claimed that the company it advertised 'had sold more T-28's than anyone else except North American Aviation'. Now that was quite a claim, and I decided it warranted further investigation!

Mark Clark's *Courtesy Aircraft* has sold just over 80 T-28s in the last six years. Mark adds 'We have sold more, but I'd have to dig out the records to check'. This wasn't just a number that Mark had plucked out of the air - he supplied me with a list of serials which detailed the aircraft he had handled.

In 1991 alone *Courtesy* moved several P-51s, two Wildcats, five T-6s (a total of 93 T-6s have been handled by the company over the past 20 years), A-26's, B-25's, multiples of T-34's, Corsairs, P-38 projects and many more. This is of course in addition to the large number of purely civilian aircraft the company has handled.

The growing number of T-28s has indeed been the result of an intense increase in interest in the type. One broker advertised the T-28 as 'a poor mans Hurricane'. Though not my words, and the T-28 is far from pretty, performance versus cost is obviously a bonus and we are set to see even more T-28s on the warbird market, no doubt many through *Courtesy Aircraft*........

satisfying fashion, a loud roar, a puff of smoke, the airframe shuddered and then it settled into that lovely deep radial rumbling. Sitting behind a big round engine just has to be one of life's better sensations, the slip stream tugging fiercely at your sleeve past the open canopy. Check that you have oil pressure within 20 seconds and then just relax and savour the moment. Look out at the tiny wing. After nearly eight years and 700 hours of solid Harvard flying the Yak wing really does look incredibly small. It's 30'10" span is more than 11 feet shorter that the Harvard's and I wondered if it was really up to the job. With an encouraging pat on my head Norman jumped to the ground and I was on my own.

When you're ready to taxi, signal for the chocks to be pulled clear and advance the throttle. Initially, it takes a fair amount of power to get the machine moving but, once it is, it tends to race away somewhat. Use of the brakes uses up air pressure so you need to keep your eye on the air pressure gauge, which on G-OYAK reads in Kg/cm2. The engine will foul up the plugs if it is kept at too low a power setting so the occasional burst of power is sometimes necessary to clear it. It took me a while to get the hang of taxying the aeroplane. I'm used to having no forward view on the ground so S turning was second nature, although the braking arrangement was at first quite *unnatural*. A hand operated brake lever is on the stick and controls the amount of brake pressure to be applied. Pressing either right or left rudder pedal directs that brake pressure to the corresponding drum brake on each wheel. The brakes are good and are quite capable of holding the aeroplane against full power, providing the air pressure is not below 20 kg/cm2. A gauge on the instrument panel indicates how much pressure is going to each wheel. Holding the stick back locks the tailwheel, but only if and when the aircraft is running straight. If taxying on grass the ride is quite so apparent during grass take off or landings when the speeds are above 60 knots or so. On my first couple of trips, taxying to and from the runway was by far the most demanding part of the whole exercise.

For tight radius turns the stick needs to be pushed forward quite firmly to release the tailwheel lock. The knack of manouvering the Yak on the ground comes quickly enough and shouldn't pose a serious problem to anyone.

Engine runs ups are very conventional, check that the oil temperature is above 40 degrees C, open the oil cooler and gills, power up to 2000 rpm., exercise the CSU twice not exceeding a rpm. drop of 500, check the magnetos, making sure that the mag drop is not more than 60 rpm. Pre-take off checks are fairly standard, the elevator trim being neutral for a solo flight, a half turn forward of neutral on the trim wheel if you are two up.

The take off for me was something of a disappointment. I had expected, despite being told the opposite, that with all that power the aeroplane would roar down the runway in an exhilarating surge of acceleration, pinning me to the seat. It is exciting, but mainly because the acceleration is so ponderous that you get the feeling that it isn't quite going to make flying speed before it can get airborne and the aeroplane must be positively rotated and made to unstick. I haven't tried it myself but I'm told that it will stay firmly on the ground until at least 105 knots before it makes any signs of trying to fly itself off.

The wide-track undercarriage helps a great deal on the take off roll and keeping it straight is surprisingly easy, a small amount of right rudder is all that is required to keep it anchored firmly to the centreline. The tail is gently lifted as soon as possible, normally at about 40 knots, to help the machine accelerate and again there is hardly any swing as the tail comes up. The view forward is good in the flying attitude although not as good as the Harvard due

to the extra metal work around the four windows that make up the windscreen. A reasonably firm pull is necessary to unstick the Yak from the ground and it sometimes tends to bobble slightly as it gets airborne. The gear safety catch is slid aside and the gear lever pressed in and raised to the up position. The gear travels fairly quickly up into the wheel wells in a loud hissing of air, easily heard above the roaring of the engine. The pin indicators in the wings that protrude upwards above it's surface a few inches when the gear is down, slide back into their recesses when the gear is raised. This is a useful, and, from a safety point of view, valuable second indication to the gear position at any time.

When the aeroplane is airborne it begins to take on an entirely different character, the slightly ponderous feelings of the take off giving way to a sensation of lively and crisp handling. The Yak, after my first take off accelerated well and I was amazed to find it quickly

reaching 200 knots. Before my first trip Norman had encountered a sudden left wing heaviness while flying the machine that had required a fair amount of strength to correct. We all suspected that may be one of the gear doors was floating slightly and so it was decided that I would fly past observers on the ground at a reasonably high speed to see if anything was obviously wrong with the underside. Unfortunately, by the time I was half way downwind I was deeply in love with the aeroplane. It was so beautifully responsive that I forgot the brief entirely, I roasted past the ground crew at some ridiculously high speed making nonsense of the whole exercise, pulled to the vertical, yelled with delight and rolled out north for ten minutes of serious flying. I was quite simply lost to the world and gone to heaven.

In cruise the Yak, at 60% power, uses fuel at a very economical 21 Imperial gallons per hour. This power will give you a good 170 knots. I found it an exhilarating machine to fly. Some people have made some rather unkind comments about the sound of the Yak, even likening it to an asthmatic tractor. I thought it was stunning. To me the engine roared, with all the fury of the most powerful fighters I had only ever dreamed of flying. The roll rate was simply incredible. So often in the past while displaying my Harvard I had begged and coaxed the last drop of energy from the aeroplane, never getting quite enough, and yet here I had the energy to spare. I could pull into a vertical roll and not have to worry about the speed, it was all so effortless. I could do things with ease that in my own aeroplane took a great deal of care and constant practice. In fact, I could do things that I wouldn't dare to even try in my own aeroplane. I was divorced from the earth, shouting and chuckling to myself like a man possessed. I had never enjoyed flying as much. In some ways it was almost too easy, although the machine does have some squirrelly corners lying in wait for the over confident. I think the

Harvard requires a far more delicate touch and if you are to maintain energy on that aeroplane and fly low level aerobatics successfully you have to get it *right*. The Yak is much easier to display, rarely struggling for energy, unlike the poor Harvard pilot who seems to spend every airborne minute always wanting that little bit *extra*.

The stall, when it comes, is slightly unusual, particularly if it occurs while manoeuvering the aeroplane at speed. The first sign is a tendency for the airframe to tighten itself up in the turn and for the pressure on the stick to ease off of it's own accord. Pushing forward on the stick at this stage stops the situation deteriorating any further.

If you don't take prompt recovery action the aeroplane will let loose in a quite exciting manner, although, the recovery action is the same and the recovery itself pretty much instantaneous providing the machine isn't allowed to wind itself up.

The conventional stall is less exciting, but the Yak will drop a wing quite sharply and, apart from the same stick lightening as in the accelerated stall, with very little warning.

This is a *fast* aeroplane and so needs to be brought into a busy circuit with some caution. The best way to arrive, and the most fun, is the run and break. On returning to the Duxford overhead after my first trip, I was so excited and comfortable in the Yak that to have simply landed would have been an insult to the machine for the pleasure it had just given me. Air Traffic approved a run and break and so it was most definitely game on. With about 280 knots indicated I came across the boundary at 100 feet or so and pulled up into a long, graceful barrel roll, then a quick three quarter aileron roll to turn downwind. Gear limiting speed is 145 knots but it is not difficult to slow the aircraft down to this from the break. If, while in cruise perhaps, the gear lever has been placed into the neutral position, it should first be

selected to up before being put in the down position, otherwise the gear lowers very quickly and makes a hell of a thump as it locks. Again, the air system makes itself heard with a loud hissing noise as the gear travels. Let the speed come back to 124 knots or below and the you can lower the flaps. The flaps on the Yak are either fully up or fully down with no intermediate position and cause an instant and fairly dramatic nose down change of attitude when they are lowered.

On my first landing in the Yak I had expected the airspeed to wander somewhat during the approach but I was pleasantly surprised to find it very stable. I flew the initial part of the approach at 105 knots, letting the speed bleed back to 90 as I crossed the hedge. I've seen people approach slower than that but with my very limited time on type and with a long runway ahead of me I've proceeded with some caution in this department. I'm sure that tiny wing has several surprises in store for me. The

view forward as the aircraft rolls out on finals is truly awful. The curved approach is essential for this aeroplane if you are interested in looking at the spot you wish to land on for as long as possible. The Yak tends to fall away somewhat in the last moments of the flare although with a little experience I have begun to feel for this. My first few landings were however a tad firmer than I would have wished, but, I did at least avoid bouncing merrily down the runway.

I made no attempt to three point the first landing. That sort of *finesse* could come later as far as I was concerned. All I wanted was to get it down safely and with as little fuss as possible. I touched down on the main wheels in a tail low attitude that seemed to do the trick quite nicely. I held the stick steady until I felt the tail wanting to lower itself and then simply cushioned it's contact with the runway. There was no tendency to swing at all as the tail came down. The roll out was yet another pleasant surprise, the aeroplane again staying firmly on the

centre line with only the gentlest of rudder corrections needed to keep it straight. I've got about 1250 landings in my Harvard and no ground loops so far so maybe I've been well prepared. Who knows? What I do know is that the Yak 11 is a delightful aeroplane directionally on the runway, during both the take off and landing.

Towards the end of the landing run I gently applied the brakes and turned onto the taxiway. Sliding the hood back I sat for a moment and let it all sink in. It was a milestone for me and it was certainly one in the eye for one or two other people who would probably never know or care, but I knew and I cared.

Taxying in was almost as slow and difficult as taxying out. When I later looked at the video that Norman had taken for me I noticed that I was wearing the same idiot grin that I had worn after my first ever solo many years before.

I've flown the Yak a few more times since that first trip and each time I've loved it more. I recently qualified for the group C Display Authorisation in G-OYAK, which was for me the high point of my flying so far. I'm amazed at the generosity and trust of Eddie Coventry and can't thank him and BAC *Windows* enough for letting me fly it. Norman Lees and myself will be operating the aeroplane for Eddie throughout the 1992 air display season, as well as our own *Radial Pair* (see the exclusive article in *Warbirds Worldwide* 19) formation aerobatic duo.

I must say that I believe the time I've built up flying the Harvard was invaluable in making the transition to the Yak 11 a fairly simple and enjoyable process. For anyone intending to get into big pistons I would say that the Harvard is a good machine to master before you move upwards. It is not as fast, not so powerful, or as complex as some perhaps, but it makes you work very hard until your reactions become instinctive, which they must if you are to be at ease and therefore at your best in the more powerful aircraft. I believe that I had the right balance of caution and confidence on the day that I first flew the Yak and consider it to be an excellent next step up from the Harvard.

WW Gary Numan

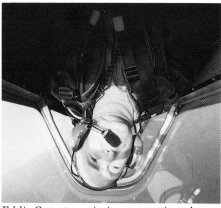

Eddie Coventry enjoying every minute!

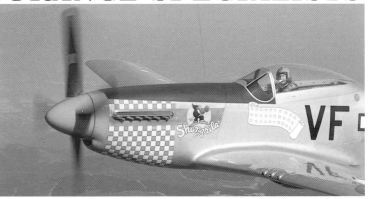
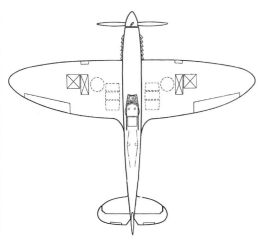

Superb Sabre

With the number of airworthy warbirds entering the UK (and the rest of Europe) growing by the month it is easy to become blase about the wealth of historic flyable aircraft on view to the enthusiast. Though the Swiss Vampire auction saw several British jets being registered the jet coup of the year has to be down to the *Golden Apple Trust* who recently imported the classic American jet - the F-86A Sabre N178 from the United States. As we go to press the aircraft is being re-assembled by *Jet Heritage*, the leading combat jet operator in Europe. It is hoped the aircraft will be seen at several UK airshows this year in line with the G.A.T.'s policy of displaying its aircraft to the public.

Built by North American Aviation (NAA) at Inglewood, California, as only the 49th production F-86A-5NA model Sabre, it was accepted by the USAF on 18th April 1949 and delivered to March AFB in California where it was formerly accepted by No. 1 Maintenance Support Group.

It was passed to Air Material Command (AMC), at the same base, on 21st April 1949, possibly for modifications and installation of military equipment not called for in the original specification given to NAA.

On 4th May 1949, 48-178 was transferred to Strategic Air Command under project SAC-122,

and was immediately assigned to 9143 Interceptor Flight for SAC bomber escort duties. The aircraft served with SAC until 2nd November 1950 when it again passed to AMC at Victorville then later Long Beach, probably for major overhaul and more modification work over a three month period.

On 2nd March 1951 48-178 was assigned to Air Defense Command, and again passed through Long Beach. Just 13 days later the aircraft was pressed into service for a short spell with the 56th Fighter Interceptor Squadron and based at Selfridge AFB.

On 2nd August 1951 '178 was assigned to the 93rd Fighter Interceptor Squadron at Kirtland AFB, New Mexico. On 20th November 1951 the Sabre was transferred to AMC at Brookley AFB. In December 1952 '178 was again transferred to ADC this time to Fresno in California.

May 11th 1954 saw the aircraft being given a new assignment with the Air National Guard and the 196th Fighter Bomber Squadron at

Paul Coggan reports on the **Golden Apple Trust's** F-86A Sabre, currently the only one flying in the world - now based in the U.K.

Ontario, California.. Though not recorded on the aircraft record card it is believed the Sabre was returned to AMC at Fresno and was stored for at least ten years before being Struck off Charge with the USAF and sold to a local reclamation yard at the same location. It remained at the local yard, largely complete, until 1970 when the remains were purchased by Ben Hall of Seattle, Washington.

Ben Hall formerly owned and raced Mustangs and T-6s Texans before acquiring the dismantled F-86A along with two other F-86As - namely 47-606/N57965 and 49-1324/N57964, the former of which was used as a spares source for 48-0178 during the extensive rebuild that followed.

When Hall purchased the aircraft it had no powerplant, no wing leading edges and the cockpit area had been stripped out completely. Another zero time engine was purchased along with a spare unit.

Assisted by Howard Mercer, Roy Lund and Rad Kostel, Ben Hall began the task of restoring 48-0178 to airworthy condition. In the spring of 1972, with the Sabre half way finished, Ben Hall decided to take on the task full time, also hiring the services of Bill Heine as an engine specialist. Additionally, help was sought from R.A. Bob Hoover, then Vice President, Special Projects at *Rockwell International*, El Segundo,

Superb Sabre

California. Hoover was for many years a test pilot on F-86s. Another North American Aviation man, Bud Snyder provided additional invaluable assistance. Nevertheless, the main task of physically rebuilding the Sabre was left to Ben Hall and his crew.

The Sabre was registered as N68388 and on May 24th 1974 with Boeing test pilot Paul Bennett at the controls 48-0178 took to the air for the first time following restoration. Airborne from Paine Field, Washington there were only a few minor problems on the aircraft's maiden flight. Ben Hall soloed in the aircraft on May 31st 1974 after a basic refresher jet course in a T-33.

In October 1983, 48-0178 was re-registered by Ben Hall as N178. It was purchased from Hall by John Dilley of *Fort Wayne Air Service* in June 1989 before the aircraft was acquired by The *Golden Apple Trust* early in 1990. Following the acquisition the aircraft was flown on several occasions by John before being surveyed. A complete overhaul and extensive work was performed by *Fort Wayne Air Service* which included reactivation of the ejection seat and extensive refurbishment, particularly in the cockpit area. Chuck Scott of the *Combat Jets Flying Museum* undertook extensive test flying of the newly restored aircraft in the autumn of 1991 and reported it 'handled like a dream' The photo-

graph opposite was taken by Eric Hayward of *Jet Heritage* who flew to the United States to further survey the aircraft and accept it on *Golden Apple's* behalf.

The aircraft was registered G-SABR in October 1991 and arrived in the UK in early January (see above photograph). It is being assembled in preparation for test flying as we go to press. N178 will be available for a limited number of airshow appearances in 1992. For further information and to book the F-86 for airshows please contact Adrian Gjertsen on 081 874 1572. **WW Paul Coggan.**

Tom Wood's Peruvian Sabre

Recovered from Peru in February 1981 by the late David Žeuschel of *Zeuschel Racing Engines* fame along with another aircraft (51-2988) North American F-86F 52-5139 was the 834th production F-86F-30NA of a batch of 858 aircraft of the dash 30NA variety. The prototype F-86F first flew on 19th March 1952. It has a wingspan of 39 feet 1 inch (two feet longer than the A model though the F fuselage is 6 inches shorter !) and is powered by the General Electric J47-GE-27 developing 5970lbs s.t. (as a pose to the F-86A engine which develops 5200lbs s.t.)

The Sabre arrived from Peru in February 1981 and was rebuilt to flying condition, being registered as N86F in June the same year. The late John R. Sandberg owned the aircraft for a brief spell before it passed to the *Exotics Leasing Corporation* of Santa Barbara, California and then *Aviation Systems International* of Van Nuys in 1987.

The North American Aviation Sabre (and it's Canadair counterpart, has become increasingly popular as a jet warbird over the last five or so years. Since the early 1980's South America has become the source of several later model Sabre's, particularly Peru and Argentina who have operated the type as a front line fighter. Of course *Flight Systems* have operated a large number of Sabres for many years, and these may eventually come onto the warbird market.

Additionally there have been a number of the more powerful Avon engined aircraft imported into the USA from Australia and Indonesia.

Heritage Aircraft Sales of Indianapolis, Indiana acquired 52-5139 in February 1989 and it is flown by *Warbirds Worldwide* member Tom Wood. Since being flown by Tom it has appeared at several airshows in an immaculate polished metal state. It evokes excitement wherever Tom takes it. It was photographed here by Robert S. DeGroat high above the state of Wisconsin during EAA's Oshkosh 1991.

Eric Hayward captured Golden Apple's F-86A with Chuck Scott at the controls during post refurbishment test flying **(Opposite page top)** *It makes an interesting contrast with the later model F-86F operated* **(illustrated directly opposite)** *by Tom Wood (Bob DeGroat Photo).*

Good Fortune & Jet Warbirds

Here I am. Headed downwind with the boards out. Another dazzling performance but I've still got to land this thing. The folks expect a greaser and that's just what they'll get. Turning for the ninety. Gear down. Flaps coming. Good wing pins. Three green. Hydraulic and pneumatics good. Gear handle neutral and double *check three green*. Cleared to land. On centreline. Good speed. A little flare and idle power. Smooth as a baby's back side. Gently lower the nose and... what's this? My chin's on the ground and the sparks are flying! Nose gears collapsed, no problem. Keep her straight. Fuel lever off, battery and generator off. Slow enough for brakes. Easy on the brakes. I'll coast into the long field cable but no matter. Stopped. Out of here! Pretty good job right? Not quite.

I jump to the ground and run up front, expecting to see two mangled gear doors, who knows what else. What I find is bitter-sweet. The sweet is that the doors are tucked snugly against the fuselage and the entire nose is suspended above the concrete by what's left of a 37mm cannon barrel - no other visible damage.

The bitter is that it starts to dawn on me that a collapsed nose gear would have put at least partially opened doors on the runway, that the undamaged doors meant that the gear wasn't down to begin with and that I missed it. I screwed up. Never mind hardly any damage. I was lucky. How did I miss it? Stuff happens. It usually happens to the other guy but sometimes it happens to you. Sometimes it happens because of your direct input - you perform an action, realise you've made an error and make a correction. Sometimes it's a surprise - a system fails, a commuter suddenly fills your

Doug Schultz shares his experience of an undercarriage failure in a MiG-17 and outlines some general guidelines to get the best from your performance!

windscreen or a tyre blows - now you have to react in a timely and decisive manner. Either way, with or without your initiative, and sometimes because you're unaware, inattentive or downright negligent, stuff happens. And it happens *faster* in jets.

After nearly 15,000 total hours over 5,000 in tactical jets, I'm here to report that I owe my continued survival to a - not always equal combination of skill and plain good fortune - good fortune being just another term of good luck. Most of the time a higher level of skill might have contributed more to the outcome of a particular flight, but I can look back and recall that sometimes I felt luckier than good.

If you find yourself smiling at my notion of luck, think again. We're flying very sophisticated ex-military machinery at often high performance levels. Most of these aeroplanes were not designed performance levels. Most of these aeroplanes were not designed for shirt sleeved strolls down Victor airways. They were built for combat or to train people for combat.

At speeds equalling and sometimes more than doubling those of their World War II piston counterparts, these aeroplanes are every bit as exciting as they are potentially unforgiving and deadly. They do not distinguish a battle hardened veteran from a surgeon turned jet enthusiast. They don't care that you're manning up for fly-bys at an airshow instead of going

to war. At a minimum, you still have to get safely airborne, operate essential systems, perform basic to high performance manoeuvres and get back on the ground - all discounting the possibility of anything from a simple malfunction to a critical action emergency, much less an error in recognition, judgement or execution.

When we consider advancing age, systems complexity and performance capabilities, and the higher speeds and compresses reaction times of our operations, we're lucky when nothing goes wrong. There is an old saying among military pilots - one that applies to any activity involving physical risk: "I'd rather be lucky than good."

Somewhere in the pages of the volumes that this statement speaks, it is not only implicit that if you're lucky you can still survive when everything goes wrong, but that if you're good you'll be lucky, and better you are the luckier you'll get. There are two kinds of luck: the luck that just happens and the luck we make, and dependence on the first kind is not the way to promote longevity in aviation, let alone in jet warbirds. Next time, I'll share some thoughts about manufacturing your own luck. Luck is more than good fortune - it is also preparation meeting opportunity.

Editors note: Doug is a Vietnam War veteran in Navy Phantoms. With his partner, Lee Lauderback, he conducts dual training in the TF-51 Mustang *Crazy Horse*, flies high performance airshow demonstrations in their Mig-17, and instructs students from the Naval and Air Force Test Pilots Schools in the MiG 21U operated by *Warplanes, Inc.*

Aggressive Gnat?

*Lance Aircraft Supply's Gnat (featured in Warbirds Worldwide Number 14) has recently had a complete overhaul, with extensive work being completed on the cockpit and exterior paint job. Morey Darznieks reports that he purchased the spares held by the Morgan Merrill and N513X has been fitted with all new panels and fillets - plus the cockpit area has been completely refurbished. To finish the job the aircraft has been painted in an Aggressor type three tone blue paint scheme. the aircraft was stripped, etched, alodined, three coat primered and base coated before the various colours and a coat of clear was applied. **This excellent Gnat is for sale - you can contact Morey on (214) 247 3701 or fax him on (214)406 0419.**

Grumman Hellcat Update

Michael Shreeve details the latest happenings on the Hellcat front and produces a list of the survivors promised in WW17.

Since the article in WW 16, the main news on the Hellcat front has concerned the UK. The Fighter Collection's 80141, now on the British Civil Register as G-BTCC, has been repainted as Alex Vraicu's F6F-3 40467 of VF-16. Substantial portions of this actual aircraft, ex Victory Air Museum, were incorporated into the rebuild of 801141 (then registered as N100TF) after it's force landing on a road and subsequent substantial airframe damage in 1979. The aircraft in it's new paint scheme, was the undoubted star of Duxford's Classic Fighter Display in July 1991, where the guest of honour was Alex Vraicu himself. A modest man, but with many new friends on this his first visit to the UK, and professed himself to be impressed at the standards of workmanship of the Fighter Collection engineers.

Besides 80141, the UK now boasts a second airworthy Hellcat, with the arrival of 79863 (pictured on p.46 of WW 16). This aircraft has been acquired by *Warbirds of Great Britain* and shipped to the UK, where it joins the impressive collection being assembled at Biggin Hill and Bournemouth. This brings the UK's Hellcat population to three (including the Fleet Air Arm Museum's static example).

In the USA, the main news has been the continuation of the rebuild of the Weeks Air Museum's example (a rare F6F-3) to flying condition in his workshops at Tamiami, Florida. This will join the four other examples now flyable in the USA: Bob Pond's, the *Kalamazoo Air Museum's*, *Planes of Fame's* and *Lone Star Flight Museum's* F6F-5s. A further airworthy example, an F6F-3 is currently owned by the *Champlin Fighter Museum*, at Mesa in Arizona The list of surviving Hellcats (21 in all) is believed to be the most complete and accurate yet published.

Bu No	Civil Reg.		Status
F6F-3			
●41476	N41476	USMC Museum, Quantico, Virginia	**Museum**
●41834		NASM Washington, DC	**Museum**
●41930	N103V	Champlin Fighter Museum, Mesa, Arizona	**Museum**
●42874		San Diego Aerospace Museum (Wreckage from sea bad)	**Museum**
●43014	N7537U	Weeks Air Museum, Tamiami, Florida	**Rebuilder**
●66237		Pima County Air Museum, Arizona (wreckage from sea bed)	**Museum**
F6F-5			
●77722		Naval Headquarters, Andrews AFB, Maryland.	**Displayed**
●78645	N9265A	Charles Nichols, Baldwin Park, CA.	**Stored**
●79192		Bradley Air Museum, Windsor Locks, Conneticut	**Museum**
●79593		U.S.S. Alabama Memorial, Mobile, Alabama	**Museum**
●79683	N4PP	Kalamazoo Air Zoo, Michigan	**Airworthy**
●79779	(KE209)	Fleet Air Arm Museum, Yeovilton	**Museum**
●79863	N79863	Warbirds of Great Britain, Biggin Hill	**Airworthy**
●80141	G-BTCC	The Fighter Collection, Duxford. (contains major parts of 40467)	**Airworthy**
●80166	N1078Z	Confederate Air Force, Midland, Texas.	**Stored**
●93879	N4994V	Air Museum, Chino, California.	**Airworthy**
●94203	(N7865C)	U.S. Naval Museum, Pensacola, Florida.	**Museum**
●94204	N4998V	Lone Star Flight Museum, Galveston, Texas	**Airworthy**
●94263		USMC Mus. (loaned Cradle of Aviation Museum, Garden City, NY)	**Museum**
●94385	N7861C	Mike Coutches, Hayward, California (wreckage, ex CAF)	**Stored**
F6F-5			
●94473	N4964W	Bob Pond, Minneapolis, MN	**Flyable**

Classic Fighter Shapes Up

Paul Coggan gets in an early preview of Duxford's Classic Fighter Air Display and tells **YOU** why you should support it in 1992.

Duxford in February is a very different place to the Duxford we know in July. For a start it is so much quieter. At least *outside* the hangars. Put your head inside the accommodation of the resident warbird operators this time of year and you will see what warbirds are really all about. I will no doubt be accused by some of *harping* on about the supreme sacrifice made by the operator's engineers this time of year. When you and I are sat in a nice warm office banging away at the keyboard the engineers are banging away at something completely different and freezing their backsides off working on aeroplanes. Warbirds.Well perhaps not all that much banging, but rather engineering in the true sense of the word. It has always seemed odd to me that our American friends (and, seriously, I don't want that to sound patronising) call their aeroplane engineers Airplane *mechanics*.

For me there is a strange fascination in a machine laying in pieces undergoing 'winter maintenance'. And yet many people truly do not appreciate the vast effort (putting the expense aside)involved in putting a warbird into the air, demonstrating it for a whole year (as it should be demonstrated) and keeping it there! We should of course show our appreciation by dipping our hands in our pockets and going to the *Classic Fighter Air Display*. Not just one day. B*ut both*. You are bound to miss something on the first day. Small price to pay to witness the sight of a lifetime. It really is easy to become blase about warbirds with such an impressive line up and even potential participation from outside the U.K. As true enthusiasts I think we owe it to everyone currently working on warbirds and the CFAD at Duxford to turn up and support the event! T*his is a show being organised for* YOU!

The *Classic Fighter Air Display* (note the new name for 1992) is set to move to a two day event this year and things are already shaping up for it to be another phenomenal show. Scheduled to take place on **Saturday 4th and Sunday 5th July 1992** the air display will have 'a significant American theme to commemorate the 50th Anniversary of the U.S. Forces' arrival in the UK' according to a spokesman at the Imperial War Museum. *Good News* for those planning to attend is that **tickets are available in advance** this year, largely as a result of public demand. The in advance prices make the show *supreme* value for money at £6.50 Adults, £4.50 OAP's and £3.00 for children (each day of course). On *the day* prices are £8.00 for adults,

An Ace plus Three. Captain Jack Ilfrey beside his P-38, bearing the symbols for eight victories. Note the symbols for two locomotives (Courtesy The Fighter Collection)

£6.00 OAP's and £4.00 for children, even then still excellent value for money. We certainly applaud the organisers for the children's rate - it would be very rewarding to see large numbers of youngsters enjoying the warbirds show (and it takes the attention away from the real kids - us!)

So what can you expect to see at the *Classic Fighter Air Display* this year? The *Fighter Collection* P-38 will be here, and the *Old Flying Machine Company's* Fury will also be on hand as a newcomer and we look forward to seeing Mark Hanna fly it. Also on the newcomers front the Spitfire XIV (G-SPIT) is expected to fly with two Mk IXs and a PR.11. Slightly heavier but of equal attraction is the *Fighter Collection* Skyraider (one of the Editor's favourite display aircraft) as well of course as the now resident unique Bf 109 Trop. The *Battle of Britain Memorial Flight* are also

expected to attend in force and other significant types include Corsairs, Mustangs, P-47 Thunderbolt and Kittyhawk, Hurricane, Hunter, Avenger and the British Aerospace Mosquito, which by then will probably have a new paint scheme. For those people that need a heavy dose of jet noise there will be a Phantom, F3 Tornado and the *Red Arrows* (who might just pick up a few tips on how to fly formation in real aeroplanes from the resident operators!). There will of course be lots of activity on the ground including the *Warbirds Worldwide* stand complete with your resident sun tanned (burned) Editor who will be only too pleased to meet you. Many USAAF veterans are expected to attend the two day event, making it an even more special occasion.

One of the people we hope will be there is Jack Ilfrey, veteran P-38 and P-51 Mustang Ace.

Jack is not only an accomplished Ace but a real character. Born in Houston, Texas, he attended Texas A&M before signing up with the USAAC, with which he served two tours of combat in the European and Mediterranean theatres, flying 142 Combat Missions and 528 Combat Hours. He was in the 94th Hat in the Ring Fighter Squadron (of World War I fame), First Fighter Group and was the first Ace of the 94th, scoring his fourth and fifth victories the day after Christmas, 1942. Heavily decorated Jack holds the Air Medal, with twelve Oak Leaf Clusters, Distinguished Flying Cross with Silver Oak Leaf Cluster, Silver Star and European and African Theatre Ribbons with six Bronze stars. The significance of all this? As a special tribute to Jack, Stephen Grey has elected to paint the *Fighter Collection's* P-38 in the colours of one of Jack's aircraft, *Happy Jack's Go Buggy*. A tribute indeed. WW *Paul Coggan.*

Advance Tickets and Information Available from the IWM on 0223 835000.

Help get a Bristol Fighter F2b Back into the air!

Another Classic Fighter we can to look forward to seeing is The Fighter Collection's Bristol F2b currently undergoing restoration at Skysport. Ex RFC serial F4516 is Britain's oldest surviving registered fighter, on the U.K. register as G-ACAA. The Fighter Collection are asking for your help to locate a Rolls-Royce Falcon engine, a scarfe ring, Lewis Gun and a Vickers Gun. If you can help please call them on 0223 834973 or Fax 0223 836956. Alternatively you can write to: The Fighter Collection, Duxford Airfield, Cambs CB2 4QR England.

HOT OFF THE PRESS - AVAILABLE NOW

Warbirds Today Series No.2

MUSTANGS

84 Pages - 32 in full Colour

Just a *small selection* of the features included:

■ **PIONEER AERO**

Elmer Ward explains the philosophy behind building modern day Mustangs at Pioneer's facility at Chino. Exclusive Photography by *Joe Cupido*

■ **INITIAL IMPRESSIONS**

Norman Lees takes to the air for his first solo in a P-51D in the United States. Intrepid Aviation Mustang photography by *John Dibbs*

■ **AN AFFAIR WITH *LADY JO***

Paul Coggan flies out of Chino, California, with Daryl Bond in his TF-51D. Photography by *Joe Cupido*

■ **ONE MAN'S PLEASURE**

Paul Coggan takes a look at Butch Schroeder's unique F-6D variant currently on rebuild at Danville, Illinois. Mike VadeBonCoeur took the photographs.

■ **THE FRENESI CONNECTION**

Robert S. DeGroat details the rebuild of Jim Beasley's ex Dominican Mustang in the U.S.A. and the story behind its striking paint scheme.

■ **ADJUSTING MY ATTITUDE**

Derek Macphail reports from Florida, the home of *Stallion 51's* Mustang training programme run by *Lee Lauderback* and *Doug Schultz.*

■ **DOUBLE TROUBLE TWO - EASTBOUND**

Christian Schweizer writes about the ferrying of P-51D N51EA from Nashua, New Hampshire to its new home in Switzerland. *Erich Gandet* Colour Spread

■ **TRI-STATE AVIATION INC.**

Paul Coggan interviews Gerry Beck and examines the Mustang and sub-assemblies being made at this North Dakota Facility. Photography by *Dick Phillips* and *Brian Silcox.*

■ **AIRWORTHY EUROPEAN MUSTANGS**

James Kightly and *Gary Brown* look at the steadily increasing Mustang population in Europe.

WARBIRDS TODAY SERIES

MUSTANGS

REBUILDING & FLYING THE NORTH AMERICAN AVIATION P-51 IN THE 1990's

WARBIRDS
WORLDWIDE

Prices (Airmail Overseas):
UK £8.95 (plus £1.50 P&P), Rest of Europe £8.95 (plus £2.50 P&P) USA $15.95 (plus $4 P&P) CANADA C$17.00 (plus $4 P7P), AUSTRALIA $18.00 (Plus $4.00 P&P). NEW ZEALAND $25.00 (Plus $4.00 P&P)

Order Yours Today - Write, Phone or Fax

WARBIRDS WORLDWIDE, P.O. Box 99, Mansfield, Notts NG19 9GU ENGLAND
Tel: (0623) 24288   Fax (0623) 22659

Bob Pond's Practical Warbird

Frank Mormillo examines the practicality of Bob Pond's Douglas AD-5W Skyraider rebuilt by Steve Hinton's **Fighter Rebuilders.**

O f all the true heavy metal warbirds flying today, the most practical (if such a thing can be said about warbirds at all) is probably the Douglas AD-5 fat-faced *Spad*. Just now finding it's way onto the warbird scene, this versatile version of the famous and rugged Skyraider line, with only one (although rather big) engine to feed, can comfortably accommodate two pilots and four passengers under it's cavernous canopy. If someone really wanted to push it, space could probably be found in the aft fuselage for another four or more passengers without getting anywhere near the aircraft's load-lifting limit.

Developed in 1951, the AD-5 was a radical modification of the basic single-seat Skyraider design intended to accommodate a two man crew side-by-side. The aircraft's fuselage was widened and lengthened and a completely new canopy and windscreen were installed. To counteract the change in the centre of gravity, the aircraft's uprated R-3350-26W radial engine was moved forward eight inches and the vertical tail surfaces were increased in area by 50 per cent to improve directional stability.

Considered to have been the most versatile Skyraider variant, the AD-5 was used for night attack, electronic warfare, airborne early warning and anti-submarine missions. Carrying as

many as four crew members for some of it's combat missions, the aircraft's great load-lifting capability and internal volume made it possible fit additional passengers of cargo in the fuselage for carrier on board delivery (COD) duties as well.

Initially used by the U.S. Navy and Marine Corps, the AD-5 version of the Skyraider was eventually used by the USAF and the Vietnamese Air Force as well, under the A-1E designation (Navy versions in service then also received the new designation). In the age of supersonic jets, the venerable *Spad* still proved to be extremely useful for close air support and helicopter escort missions during the Vietnam War. Flying solo at the time, one A-1E pilot, USAF Major Bernard Fisher, earned the Medal of Honour by landing his *Spad* on an abandoned airstrip under heavy enemy fire to rescue a comrade who had been shot down. After scrambling into the vacant right seat, the rescued pilot and

Fisher escaped unharmed. This Skyraider also survived the war and is now on display at the Air Force Museum as a unique Medal of Honour aircraft exhibit.

At last count, after four decades of service, at least 47 Skyraiders airframes are believed to be in existence and 21 were on the U.S Civil Aircraft Register as of 30 June 1990. One of the most recent Skyraiders to have been restored to flying condition is Bob Pond's *Planes of Fame East* AD-5W (EA-1E), which was built at Steve Hinton's *Fighter Rebuilders* crew at Chino, California and took to the air again on 8 July 1991. Now registered as NX188BP, this Skyraider had been in open storage for 20 years before Mr. Thomas Stafford brought it to Chino and eventually sold it to Bob.

Assigned Navy Bureau Number 135188, Pond's Skyraider was originally accepted by the U.S.N. from Douglas at El Segundo, California on 23 June 1955 and assigned to VC-11 NAS North Island, California. During the next four and a half years, the Skyraider served aboard the U.S.S. *Wasp* (CV-18), the U.S.S. *Hornet* (CV-

Steve Hinton at the controls of the huge Skyraider, BuNo 135188/N188BP which was in open storage for some 20 years before being purchased by Thomas Stafford who eventually sold it to Bob Pond at Planes of Fame East.

12) and the U.S.S. *Shangri La* (CV-38) between shore assignments before being placed in storage at Litchfield Park, Arizona on 29 December 1959.

On 30 November 1962, the Skyraider was redesignated EA-1E while still in storage and stricken from the books in March 1963. However, with the U.S. involvement in the Vietnam War, it was reinstated into service and overhauled at Quonset Point, Rhode Island before being assigned to VAW-33. Subsequently serving aboard the U.S.S. *Intrepid* (CV-11) and the U.S.S. *Wasp*, the aircraft was overhauled again in March 1966, when it's radome was removed and the airframe modified and redesignated A-1E.

Initially assigned to VA-122 (an A-1 replacement training squadron) at N.A.S. Lemoore, California, it later served aboard the U.S.S. *Kittyhawk* (CV-63) and then went to VAQ-33 at Quonset Point as a utility and training aircraft. .The Skyraider was finally sent to the Military Aircraft Storage and Disposition Centre (MASDC) at Davis Monthan AFB, Arizona on 4 February 1970.After being struck from the records on 5 February 1970, it was transferred to the *Naval Weapons Centre*, China Lake, California where it remained in open storage until being acquired by Stafford in May 1989.

Commenting on it's remarkably good condition after so many in open storage, Hinton said: 'It's really great aeroplane; there were no signs of fatigue and it doesn't appear to have been heavily used by the Navy'. According to Hinton, it appears that the Navy only put about 50 hours on the airframe after the aircraft's last military overhaul.

Not very much slower than single seater Skyraiders in spite of it's bigger fuselage (top speed of the AD-5 is listed as 329 mph at 15,200 feet), the AD-5 nevertheless does handle a bit differently from it's more streamlined counterparts. Even with the enlarged vertical tail, Hinton reports that directional stability is a bit less and there is a tendency to wallow about in a bit of turbulence. Yet, he also says that it carries a load so well that it's hard to detect any difference in performance whether the aircraft is full loaded or empty.

Burning 90 gallons per hour at 200 mph on cross-country trips, Hinton says that 'It's real practical for taking maintenance and display crews on airshow trips.' Seated behind the pilots, the four passengers immediately behind the pilots facing aft.Trying to sell potential bidders on the practicality of another AD-5, the auctioneer at the recent *Santa Monica Museum of Flying Auction* described this version of the Skyraider as a family warbird. Perhaps that really is the best way to persuade doubting spouses that warbirds can be practical.**WW**
Frank Mormillo

Bottom:Fighter Rebuilders rebuilt Bob Pond's AD-5W Skyraider seen above at their workshops. Above: Steve Hinton flying Bob Pond's Douglas AD-5W Skyraider near Chino, California shortly after the aircraft's restoration to flying condition. He generally flew the Skyraider with a full load of passengers (two pilots and four people in the back) to explore it's handling qualities with a load.

Chuck Cabe's Aviation Electronics

Frank Mormillo reports on Chino's resident electronic wizard; beneath the glossy paint are some pretty complex electronics...

When warbirds like Bob Pod's AD-5W Skyraider are restored to flying condition, the aircraft owners and the restoration firms get a well deserved amount of credit for their hard work and ingenuity. However, often lost in the glare of the limelight are the various sub-contractor specialists who also lend their expertise to those projects and without whose services the safe completion of those aircraft could very well be in doubt. One such individual is Chuck Cabe who operates *Cabes-Aviation Electronics* at the Chino Airport in southern California.

'We couldn't do without him, he's the best in the business,' said John Muszala who operates *Pacific Fighters* at Chino. It was Muszala's idea to write an article about Cabe for *Warbirds Worldwide*.

Working exclusively on warbirds, Cabe has been operating out of the old *Aero Sport* hangar at Chino since December 1989. Before that, he worked as an aviation electronics specialist with other aviation maintenance and restoration firms at Chino and the Long Beach Airport. So far, he has rewired and installed electronics in 207 aircraft - everything from Stearman biplane trainers to F-86 Sabre jet fighters.

'I rewire warbirds and install today's type electronics in the aircraft so that they can conform to current FAA regulations'. Cabe said. 'Frank Sanders got me started in the business in 1974 at Long Beach when I worked in general aviation radio shops' he added. Before then, Cabe picked up a great deal of aviation electronics experience in the U.S. Army. A veteran of three tours of duty in Vietnam (including one with the *Green Berets*) as well as service in Germany, Cabe joined the Army out of high school and spent eight and one half years on active duty before returning to civilian life.

His first civilian jobs were with *Air Radio* in Broomfield, Colorado and *Denver Avionics* in Denver, Colorado before he decided to move to Long Beach, California in 1974. Cabe met Sanders at Long Beach while installing radios in Frank's T-34 Mentor and he's been in the warbird avionics business ever since. He began to work with Bruce Goessling's *Unlimited Aircraft* Company at Chino in June 1977 (Sanders had also relocated to Chino around that time) and in August 1979, Chuck moved himself and his family (he and his wife Cindy have a son, Tony, 22 and a daughter, Shannon, 19) to Chino so that he could be closer to his work and his

Chuck Cabe in his typical working environment - this time it's the cockpit of a TF-51D Mustang that was built up by Elmer Ward at Pioneer Aero. (Frank Mormillo)

expanding list of clients, most of whom came from word of mouth references.

'I miss my old buddy Frank', Cabe said while reminiscing about his years at Chino and his friendship with Frank Sanders who died in the crash of the *Red Knight* T-33 Silver Star in May 1990. Cabe does all the wiring on the Smokewinder systems that *Sanders Aircraft* still produces for military and civilian airshow work and he has been a member of the *Sanders Aircraft Dreadnought* air racing team ever since it started. Although Cabe goes to Reno every year primarily to work on *Dreadnought*, his services are in great demand by everyone and he reports that he has worked on most of the other air racers as well.

'I love what I do', Cabe said. 'Most of my cus-

tomers are pretty good and the only down side to the business is when somebody like Frank dies unexpectedly'. Further describing his work, Cabe said, 'Each job's a little different. Every customer wants something done his particular way; but we still conform to all the FAA rules and regulations. I don't do it fast. I don't do it slow. I do it right. When I'm dealing with somebody's life, I don't take any chances. If they're in a rush, I tell them to take the job elsewhere.

As far as elsewhere is concerned, it's actually Chuck who often winds up going elsewhere. His reputation is now so widespread that out of state warbird owners even fly him around the southwest to work on their aircraft, He's been to Texas to work on Jim Robinson's *Combat Jets Flying Museum* F-86 Sabre, to Arizona to work on Mike Dillon's TT-1 Pinto and he often goes to the Van Nuys Airport in California to work on Chuck Thornton's collection of jets.

Among the one of a kind aircraft that Cabe has worked on are: The *Air Museum Planes of Fame* Japanese Mitsubishi A6M5 Zero, Australian collector Guido Zuccoli's Italian Fiat G-59-B fighter -trainer and the Australian Commonwealth CA-13 Boomerang fighter-bomber that was recently built up by Dennis Sanders and Dale Clarke.

Of all his projects so far, Cabe said that Thornton's first T-38 Talon supersonic jet trainer was the most intimidating."That involved a lot more in the way of modern jet electronics." he said. According to Cabe, every thing in the jet was AC instead of DC and he had to supplement the jet's military UHF radio systems with civilian VHF systems as well as put in dual NAVs (the T-38 only had TACAN before).

"We did everything that was needed for the jet to operate safely in civilian TCAs while still leaving the military UHF gear in place for Thornton's military contracts." Cabe reported. "We adapted everything into the instrumentation that was already in the aircraft and kept a stock look in the cockpit." he added.

Generally available for his customers at Chino from 8 a.m. until 8 p.m. six days a week, Cabe does try to get home a bit earlier on Fridays and Saturdays when usually leaves the shop sometime around 5 p.m. His current projects include: A TF-51D Mustang, an F8F-2 Bearcat, a B-25 Mitchell, a Hawker Sea Fury, a T-34 Mentor, a T-28 Trojan, an F-86 Sabre and an F-5 Tiger.

"We're getting into the later types of warbirds like T-28s, F-86s and Skyraiders these days," Cabe said. Looking toward the future of the warbird industry, he stated: "Somewhere out there, there's always a barn or storage room where people keep finding old aeroplanes. If they could return all the stuff from the oceans, there would be a lot more. The future looks bright provided that the FAA and the insurance companies don't create too many problems."

When asked to comment about Cabe's work, warbird rebuilder and air racer Steve Hinton said "He's the best electronics man I've ever seen in my life. He does thorough work, his wire bundles are perfect and he's reliable. You can always tell a Chuck Cabe job by his attention to detail. He's not just a guy who can hook up wire A to wire B, he can figure out all kinds of military and civilian hook-ups, spend two months on a project and, when he's done, he turns it on and it all works. He's a breath of fresh air. **WW Frank Mormillo**

Just one of the aircraft that Chuck cabe has fitted out. As we go to press this TF-51D which was rebuilt for Warbirds of Great Britain by Pioneer Aero also located at Chino is arriving in the U.K. for the former company. Other aircraft that Chuck has equipped include a Bearcat and Guido Zuccoli's Fiat G-59 and Boomerang project. Joe Cupido Photograph. More photographs (air to air and colour) of the TF-51D can be seen in the Warbirds Worldwide work on the Mustang: Warbirds Today Number Two: MUSTANGS, an advertisement appears on Page 33.

VINTAGE PROPS & JETS Inc.

Derek Macphail reports on **Tom Crevasse's** warbird restoration facility in Florida.

Harry Doan's immaculate T-33A 58-0697 now registered N49239 (Derek Macphail)

The East coast of Florida abounds in holiday resorts enjoying the good weather that is typical of this part of America. One of these resorts is New Smyrna Beach with it's beach front properties, while just in from the coast is a former Naval Air Station now simply called New Smyrna Beach Airport. This airport, despite the tranquil air that exists about it, is the home of an organisation called *Vintage Props & Jets*, Inc. run by Tom & Linda Crevasse.

To the warbird aviation enthusiast the name of Tom Crevasse is well know as he and his restoration team have produced many fine warbird restorations; they've received many prizes to prove it! I recently paid a visit to Tom to see for myself why this man and his team have achieved so much success with warbirds. I now understand why!

I arrived at the airport and eventually found Tom's hangar that carried a modest sign with his business name on the door. As I walked from the car park towards the hangar I passed a couple of young men talking about their flying experiences. What else is there to talk about in this environment!

On entering the building I saw some offices, a couple of tables with some people preparing for a flight, and the only aircraft was a Sikorsky H-5H helicopter, Air Force serial 91999.

Flags of various nations decorate the hangar, each representing the home of his students, past and present. The lower cost of flying in the United States and the good weather are a great benefit to the student.

In reception I found Linda Crevasse who looks after the administration of the Flight School as well as the day to day running of the business. This allows Tom to concentrate on the restoration and maintenance of aircraft for which he has become well known. Linda advised me that Tom was 'on the other side of the airport' and that he would be with me shortly. While waiting for Tom I spotted a sign leaning against the wall giving a 'potted history' of *Vintage Props & Jets*, Inc. From this I learned that Tom was the person who had invented and perfected the propane/oxygen simulated aircraft machine gun that many airshow followers will have both seen and heard. This man was going to be interesting to interview!

Tom duly arrived in his utility complete with obligatory warning flag attached to the back of the cab, and we adjourned to his office for a talk. The walls of his office showed his interest in warbirds with many photographs and winners plaques pertinent to Tom and his business. It had only been a few months since *Vintage Props*

and Jets, Inc. had moved to New Smyrna Beach to larger facilities from a nearby airport. The maintenance and restoration hangar was on the other side of the airport and we would have a look at this later in the day. The restoration and maintenance of warbirds is only part of Tom and Linda's business, *Vintage Props & Jets*, Inc., which with the already mentioned Flight School also includes a General Aviation maintenance facility with aircraft sales. The priority of work in the hangar varies between the restoration and maintenance of warbirds and General Aviation aircraft depending on demand and his engineers must be able to move from one type of work to another.

The team of engineers working on the aircraft can be as many as fifteen depending on the workload and restoration projects on hand at any time. Sometimes the engineers are younger than the aircraft that they are working on but Tom's demanding standards for a high level of workmanship make sure they deliver the goods. A case in point was a small riveting job that had been carried out on a warbird restoration by a young engineer using sound aeronautical practices but using a non period style of rivet that when inspected by Tom had to be riveted with the correct period style rivets. I guess the motto must be 'if you are going to do something, do it 100% correctly'. This is why he has produced so many winners!

I asked Tom where he thought the warbird movement was going. He replied that it was going to move towards more and more jets while the area of warbird helicopters has been neglected. He sighted a Lockheed T-33 that now sells for $175,000 to $180,000 in flying condition with a cheap and plentiful source of spare parts when compared with the big piston engined Warbirds. A North American F-86 Sabre in better times would be in the $300,000 to $400,000 price market but is also a great airshow crowd pleaser because they are not overly plentiful. When did you last see a F-86 flying? It takes less time to restore a T-33 nowadays

than it does a T-6/Harvard.

Tom's background in aviation is that of a pilot with over 20,000 hours of flying behind him on more than 150 different types of aircraft. His engineering skills and the standard that he demands from his workers has insured that he enjoys an excellent working relationship with the F.A.A. and he has never had any problems regarding the issue of Aircraft Original Certificates of Airworthiness and he has been responsible for a lot of them being issued.

I was curious to know about all the types of aircraft that Tom had flown and whether he had a favourite. After some reflection he said that he had no real favourite, each aircraft having it's good and less pleasing traits giving no outstandingly good aircraft or a disastrously poor aircraft. Each one had by it's very nature had to be a compromise of design. He later said that he thought that the dash 4 Corsair was a good pilot's aircraft while the large An-2 biplane had been the most enjoyable. The An-2 was an aircraft that had to be flown at all times but could be operated spectacularly at the slow speed end of the flight envelope. Tom considered that he had the ability to get the best out of an aircraft after only a short time and this 'talent' had also been remarked upon by other pilots.

The restoration of a warbird requires a certain amount of research. Depending on the aircraft involved this can sometimes be time consuming and expensive. Tom therefore, encourages his clients to do as much of their own research as possible. Otherwise the cost of a restoration could become excessive if Tom's team were to be involved. They will, however, guide their clients in certain directions if it is required. All this work will help to produce a restored warbird to authentic standards not only cosmetically but also technically. How else do you win so many prizes?

The overhaul of some aircraft components is carried out 'in house' while the remainder are either replaced with new, if available and subject to price or sent out for overhaul. The modern horizontally opposed engines are overhauled in the workshops while radials, V's and jets are all handled by outside organisations. The rebuild of some of these engines that in themselves can be up to 50 years old using new parts that were manufactured many years ago can put an overhaul organisation in the difficult area of 'product liability' if things go wrong and this is a minefield that Tom wishes to avoid...best left to the specialist experts.

Where is the future going to see *Vintage Props & Jets Inc.* going? A slow move away from the General Aviation work towards an expansion of the Flying School side of the business with a view to being able to offer correct warbird pilot training towards the F.A.A. Letter of Authority to fly a particular type. Tom sees this as an area of growing need within the warbird fraternity especially with the move towards jets.

It was time to visit the workshop on the other side of te airport so Tom acted as guide as I followed him on the public roads to the hangar. No short cut across the airport for me! On entry to the hanger complex we passed several hangars containing some very interesting aircraft belonging to Harry Doan of *Doan Helicopters*, Daytona Beach, Florida, who was having a Sikorsky S-51 Helicopter, Coast Guard serial 203, restored in Tom's workshops. This machine was being worked on as time allowed and already the tailboom had been overhauled and painted while the transmission gearbox had also been rebuilt. The workmanship was a joy to see but I was later to be show even more proof why this workshop is truly a 'Birthplace of Champions'

Tom apologised for there not being too many warbird projects in his workshop for me to look at during my visit. However he said he would arrange for me to have a look at two of the Champions that he had restored if he could contact their owner. While he was on the telephone trying to arrange my viewing I had a look around his facilities and at a polished Lockheed T-33, N49239, painted as '80697', that was parked outside his hanger. This aircraft had recently passed through the workshop and was an indication of Tom's move towards jets while in the grass next to the hanger were two T-33s that were up for sale but required to be restored. In the workshop was a T-33 wing under restoration that belonged to an aircraft that is part owned by Tom.

The telephone call had been successful so it was into Tom's utility and off to another airport adorned by rows of the small hangars typical of so many American General Aviation airports. On entering one of these hangars I was initially confronted with a Convair L-13, N316LG, with it's wings folded. I had seen a photograph of one of these aircraft but did not realise just how large it really was. I then passed the aircraft to be introduced to C.R. 'Dick' Powell who owns this prize winning aircraft and a Bell 47G helicopter, N6360, restored as a H-13G helicopter.

This helicopter had been so completely restored by Tom that it even carries a Carbine in the correct mountings in the cockpit.

Shortly the hanger doors were opened and the helicopter was moved out into the sun (using an ingenuous electro-hydraulic rig), for me to photograph. I was almost speechless seeing the standard of the restoration and the pride of ownership that existed for this aircraft. Here was one very proud owner. The L-13 was equally magnificent and Tom told me about some of the problems that had arisen during the restorations that they had overcome. The L-13 had a Franklin engine that it was considered must be unique as spares were not listed for it and parts that were considered by the supplier to be applicable would not fit. It turned out to be a real one off rebuild. A zero time Beechcraft wooden laminated propeller was even found for the aircraft. (This magnificent L-13 has subsequently been sold and is now owned by former Astronaut Frank Borman).

It was soon time to return to New Smyrna Beach so after thanking C.R. 'Dick' Powell it was back in the Utility and off to the airport.

On our return to the office and Flight School I had to ask Tom about the H-5H helicopter parked in the hanger and he told me that it had been acquired via Harry Doan. It was believed to be the only survivor of the sixteen H-5H helicopters ever built and the target for the restoration is the 1993 E.A.A. *Sun'n'Fun Fly In* where I am sure based on what I have already seen of the work of *Vintage Props & Jets, Inc.* that it will be a prize winner.

My whole day with Tom made me realise that here was a man who with his team that he has gathered around has produced more Oshkosh winners than anybody else because of the high and exacting standards he sets himself.

The drive back to Orlando was spent reflecting on what I had seen that day and my thanks go out to Tom and Linda as well as to C.R. 'Dick' Powell for their time and generosity during my visit. Keep up the good work! **WW Derek Macphail.**

Top: Sikorsky Helicopter 91999 at Tom Crevasse's facility. Below: N6360, a completed Bell 47G Helicopter. Tom has built a multitude of fixed wing aircraft too including T-33s and Yak 11s. (D.A. Macphail).

Lone Star Flight Museum

Richard Paver provides an update on the latest news from the rapidly expanding Lone Star Flight Museum in Galveston, Texas.

Since the publication of my photo report on the *Lone Star Flight Museum* in the last edition of the journal, I am very pleased to say that Jim Fausz has kindly been in touch with me to provide an update on the rapidly developing scene at Galveston.

Following on from my interview with him in Texas last October I reported that *Lone Star* had a good P-40 on the top of their wanted list and indeed Jim has reported that this has now been achieved with the acquisition of Bill 'Tiger' Destefani's Kittyhawk 43-5795 / N1232N from Bakersfield in California.

This Kittyhawk will be well known to *Warbirds Worldwide* readers having been rebuilt to immaculate flying condition by Destefani in the early 1980s appearing in public for the first time at Reno in 1986 and having been actively displayed on the USA Airshow circuit since.

The picture below was taken by the author at Reno in 1986 just after Destefani had first flown it following restoration. Before it's acquisition by Destefani it had been on static display at *Harrahs Club* in Reno for nearly 20 years. Before

this it had been flown by Keith Larkin in the 1950s in connection with the operations of his *Weather Modification* Company.

The second piece of significant news supplied by Jim Fausz is that acquisition involved a trade of the *Lone Star* Spitfire XIV TZ138 to Tiger Destefani who was due to collect it from storage near Galveston on 15th January for trucking to Bakersfield and eventual restoration to airworthy condition. It has been known for sometime that Destefani has been on the look out for a Spit and he has been collecting Spitfire components at Bakersfield to aid in an eventual rebuild. This exchange therefore has been highly successful; satisfying the ambitions of both parties.

Jim Fausz also reports is that *Lone Star* is planning their second annual Museum Showcase and Open Day for May 2nd and 3rd 1992 where it is expected many visiting Warbirds will be gathered at Galveston. Additionally, a large part of the *Lone Star* Fleet on external display for enthusiasts to photograph without any barriers.

This event is planned as a follow up to their first highly successful Showcase held last year when an open invitation to all aviation minded people resulted in a fly in of 102 aircraft.

Concerning progress on other projects since my feature in *Warbirds Worldwide* 19 Jim has

when the aircraft was purchased it was approximately 50% restored already and so this timetable might not be quite as ambitious as it first seems.

Other restoration work in hand for the museum includes their Cessna A-37 67-14534 that is being rebuilt in Phoenix. Approximately 70% of the airframe work is complete; though the museum is still trying to locate some suitable engines and are aiming for a summer 92 completion date. They also have their Beech AT-11 N81Y 23724 being worked on in Winnie, Texas with the engines being rebuilt at JRS in Minneapolis. The restoration is at a very early stage and the museum have a complete set of military components including bomb bay doors to enable a totally authentic restoration!

Another very exciting and unique project, the Grumman F3F-2 (0972) is close to completion at Forth Worth with the engine again being worked on by JRS.It is expected to take to the air this year.

The final news on *Lone Star's* restoration activity is that their F4U-5 Corsair 121881 is at Breckenridge with Nelson Ezell. Work has just commenced and is at the 'tear down and analyse' stage. Jim reports that they have everything required to make a completely airworthy Corsair;however they will be embarking on a major reskinning exercise of the wings and centre section. When purchased *Lone Star* acquired this airframe without an engine; one has since been located and Jim is hoping that the spring of 1993 should see this airframe complete and ready to fly.

The remaining news from Galveston is that just after my visit last October, Jim Fausz concluded an agreement with *Continental Airways* to enable the Museum to display the *Continental Historical Society* DC-3 at Galveston for the winter on loan from it's usual base at Houston Hobby Airport. This aircraft was very enthusiastically received making a very interesting comparison to the largely ex-military collection at the museum and arousing considerable public interest.

My thanks to Jim Fausz for all this information - as I reported previously the scene at *Lone Star* is one of constant activity with new projects always appearing making it a museum well worth a visit for any *Warbirds Worldwide* readers. **WW Richard Paver.**

Curtiss P-40M 43-5795 has an interesting history. Ex RCAF 845, N1232N was sold to Vance Roberts in September 1947. It went through a succession of owners including Bell Air Services, Jerry McMullin, Davis Dusters,Clyde Mallory and the Weather Modification company of Redlands, California before being acquired By morrill Farr in March 1964. Harrah's Auto purchased it in December 1964; Bill Destefani acquired it in June 1982 (Richard Paver)

informed me that they have now taken delivery of their PBY, N3N and an A-20G (43-21709). The A-20 is the last flying Havoc of the 7,479 that Douglas built and is in excellent condition. Jim is considering making it available for immediate bookings for the 1992 Airshow season.

As previously reported *Lone Star* acquired Hurricane Mk11B CCF-96 from Len Tanner with the objective of having the aircraft finished by late summer this year. Jim has reported that

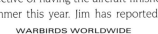

Examined a Thunderbolt cowling set lately? Don't be fooled by the external appearance - a lot of work goes into creating new sets!

For the most part, *Airframe Assemblies* are well known for their work on the Supermarine Spitfire from major assemblies - wings to other associated items in particular. Though their work in the Spitfire field has been significant and it continues the company have recently diversified with work on Hurricanes, Tempests, and Hunters amongst others. They are now in the final stages of completing a complete cowling set for the Republic P-47 Thunderbolt .

To the outsider this may seem a relatively sim-

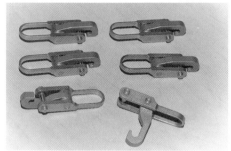

ple undertaking. However, closer investigation will reveal that this is in fact a major project. The extremely complicated cowling assembly on the P-47 consists of, to the nearest round figure, some 800 components. Add to this the fact that the available drawings were incomplete and you have an even bigger task on your hands. An American customer had asked Steve Vizard at *Airframe Assemblies* to undertake the project. By coincidence, the RAF *Museum's* Cardington based workshops were in the process of refurbishing an ex Yugoslavian P-47D and also required a replacement for the missing chin cowl on their aircraft.

Basically the construction of the cowling sets was a very major undertaking and Steve calculates it has tied two of his staff up for almost a

year. Obviously, the first production run is the most difficult, and using the drawings available plus drawings they made from available original samples *Airframe Assemblies* effectively lofted the whole set, manufacturing tooling and jigs in the process. Fortunately the company had access to the Thunderbolt at Cardington and Steve speaks highly of the co-operation they received from the RAF Museum staff in this respect. From the photographs it is obvious that the cowlings are far from from simple to manufacture. Almost all the packers, angles, gussets and major components were pressed. Even relatively straightforward top hat stringers have to be folded flat and drawn through three sets of rolls to achieve the correct contour - remember the cowls are oval shaped to further complicate matters!

this includes some of the larger skin panels - and it has been the duplication of this, manually on a wheeling machine that has taken considerable time and patience. Additionally, the stainless steel hinge points are critical, as are many other areas of the job and checking, cross checking and finalising sub component manufacture has been an exhausting process. Naturally, to tool up to press the components again would be prohibitively expensive as Steve points out, and with so few Thunderbolts undergoing restoration it would not be a cost effective proposition. However, there are several airframes in the USA that are in line for restoration and Steve makes no secret of the fact that *Airframe Assemblies* would be pleased to supply cowl sets! You can contact *Airframe Assemblies* on: 0983 404462 or Fax 0983 402806.

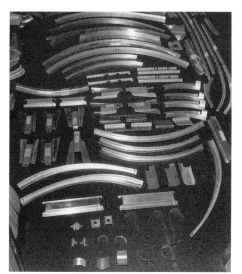

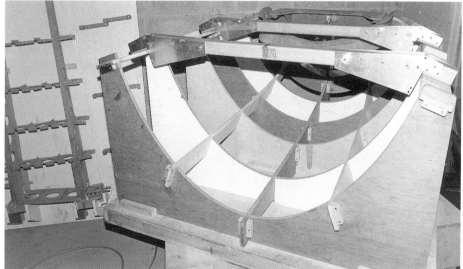

Other complex mass produced shapes had to be copied on a wheeling machine - a very difficult task indeed. As an example Steve cites one particular piece that was just two feet long and one foot wide which had some half dozen different shapes and contours incorporated into it. On the original construction there is not one panel or member that was not pressed and

The photographs (by Chris Michell) only relate to the side and top cowls - the chin cowl is an even more complex undertaking. **Top Left** *inset shows the cowling latches - a complex machining job in itself.* **Lower left** *inset - just a small(!) selection of the components.* **Main pictures - Top** *- side cowling being taken out of the build jig for.* **Lower** *the bottom cowling build jig. Airframe Assemblies have put considerable development work into these components.*

Crafting Complex Cowls

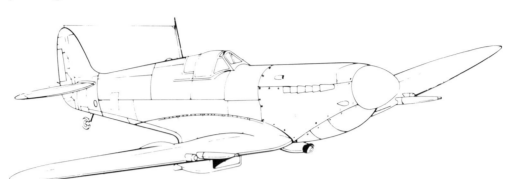

MOZAMBIQUE HARVARD

Philip Warner reports from Shoreham on the roll out of the first of several newly rebuilt Harvards. Exclusive photography by **John Dibbs**

In June 1951 under the North American charge number of NA186 design data was provided by the Columbus, Ohio division of North American Aviation to the Canadian Car and Foundry Co.(formerly Noorduyn) in Montreal under the designation T-6J. The data is similar to that of North American's well known T-6G that is a remanufactured aircraft and not a new build aircraft, which the Harvard Mark IV was.

The Harvard Mark IV also has the advantage of being built in the early 'Fifties and not under wartime pressures as most North American Texans were. A total of 555 aircraft were constructed, of which the final 285 were funded by the USAF for the Mutual Aid Programme.

Harvard serial 52-8562 was constructed in 1952 as part of the penultimate batch of 120 aircraft. This batch was supplied to West Germany before the formation of the new Luftwaffe. All except seven of the Harvards were eventually transferred to the new air force. When in Luftwaffe service '562 was painted yellow overall with the usual West German markings and coded AA + 053. One unusual feature was the cowl around the engine that was painted black at the top and bottom with black and white chequer-board sides. There was also a small area of dark green between the top of the chequer-board and the black on each side of the engine cowl.

Later '562 was transferred to a different training school and carried the code BF +053.

Andrew Edie alongside the first ex Mozambique aircraft to be rolled off the line.

Top: Norman Lees at the controls of 52-8562 airborne from Shoreham. Below: Gary Numan comes in close to the camera ship for a standard portrait shot.

In 1966 '562 was transferred to the Portuguese Air Force and carried the number 1753. It was almost certainly operated from Tancos in Portugal by a ground attack squadron after being armed with two underwing machine gun pods and bomb racks under the wings.

Five six two was then shipped to Mozambique and operated as part of the pre-independence Mozambique Air Force in what is now known as a COIN role.

Eventually, in company with many other aircraft. '562 was abandoned in the mid 'Seventies in Mozambique. In 1989, (see the full feature in *Warbirds Worldwide* Number 15) two South Africans purchased twelve Harvards from the Mozambique Government and six of these were in turn sold to Andrew Edie and John Woodhouse. 52 - 8562 is the first of the six aircraft to go through the extensive process of remanufacturing and have flown. '562 has only 2698 airframe hours recorded and is complete with a zero timed R1340 - ANI propeller.

Following purchase an impressive construction line was set up to rebuild the aircraft in tandem and Andrew set about the massive administrative task of organising the engines (from *Covington Aircraft Engines* at Okmulgee, Oklahoma - see article in *Warbirds Worldwide* 19) and a wealth of spare parts were shipped in from *Lance Aircraft Supply* in Dallas, Texas, where father and son team Morey and John Darznieks

run the leading Harvard spares supply company in the world. The projects then went ahead at a significant pace.

Having seen the quality and extent of the work undertaken by the restoration team at Thruxton it was with considerable anticipation that I drove through the pouring rain to Shoreham by Sea aerodrome in West Sussex, England to see the official roll out of the now completed Harvard Mark IV.

52-8562 was parked inside the hangar awaiting the start of proceedings. The aircraft looked absolutely immaculate in standard Royal Canadian Air Force yellow with maple leaf insignia and bearing the RCAF number 20310. In common with many other warbird restorations these days the interior was finished in light grey with black instrument panels etc. The canopy glass had all been totally replaced and looked superb.

The internal restoration involved the aircraft being completely disassembled and inspected. The wings and stabilisers were deskinned for internal cleaning, inspection, repair or replacement of parts where necessary, corrosion proofing, reassembly and painting.

The centre section had been stripped of all systems for overhaul of components including the landing gear. All components were inspected and crack tested where necessary. The systems were totally overhauled including hydraulics and fuel systems that included splitting the main fuel tanks for inspection.

All new control cables have been fitted and the electrical system including wiring have been renewed.

Flight instruments have been returned to an as new condition and all the hoses have been replaced. As mentioned previously, the R-1340powerplant and firewall forward had been overhauled by *Covington Engines*. As far as possible '562 has been returned to a stock condition.

The appearance and specification of the aircraft did confirm Mark Clark's (*Courtesy Aircraft* of Rockford, Illinois) description of the Harvard Mark IV as 'The Cadillac of the Texan/Harvard series of aeroplanes'.

Gary Numan was invited to ceremonially cut the white ribbon that lay between 562 and the apron outside the hangar. After a short speech by Andrew Edie, who mentioned all the people connected with the restoration, the ribbon was duly cut and the Harvard was then rolled out of the hangar into the weak sunshine that had now broken through.

A flying demonstration with Gary Numan flying '562 and Norman Lees in Andrew Edie's' T-6G (51-15227) then followed. The wind was over twenty knots and there was some turbulence but several formation passes were completed with '562 standing out significantly in it's new yellow paint scheme.

Both aircraft then landed and most of the

spectators retired to the bar where Andrew and John had arranged for lunch.

Andrew states that 53-8562 is still for sale at £150,000 (plus VAT where applicable). Some trades will be considered. There is considerable interest being shown in '562 and I was informed by Andrew that a further aircraft (a T-6G) can be completed in approximately twelve weeks in the customers choice of colours.

For the historians among you, one of these Harvard Mark IVs is 53-4636; the last Harvard ever built.

Our thanks to Andrew Edie and John Woodhouse for their hospitality, for allowing us access to the aircraft, and for a most enjoyable day. **WW Philip Warner**

Number One

CLASSIC FIGHTER PRINTS

Exclusive air to air photography
by John Dibbs

Number Two

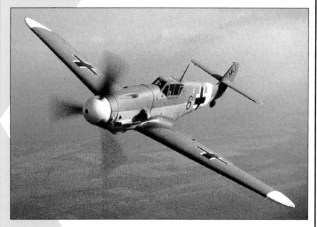

These full colour prints of the Bf109G Trop are the first in a series of new prints to be released for sale by Warbirds Worldwide. Excellent for framing, these high quality lithographic prints are available at the remarkable price. All Prices include Postage & Packing (Airmail Overseas)
Great Britain £4.95 *each* Rest of Europe £5.50 each.
United States of America $8.00 each. Canada $C8.00, Australia $10.00, New Zealand $NZ12.00. Be sure to quote which print/s you require

More to follow in the series

WARBIRDS WORLDWIDE
P.O. Box 99
Mansfield
Notts NG19 9GU
ENGLAND

WARBIRDS WORLDWIDE
TWENTY ONE

In *Warbirds Worldwide Twenty One* we catch up with the **Aircraft Restoration Company** at Duxford, Dave Clinton writes about **Aircraft Cylinder & Turbine** and Dave Clayton takes us through a jet engine rebuild at **Aero Turbine**. Graham Trant brings us smack bang up to date with the **Hurricane** front and we talk **Vampires** with a complete listing of the surviving operational aircraft including, hopefully, a list of the Swiss AF sales. We also have a pilot report on transitioning on to the **Corsair**. Jeff Ethell writes about flying the **P-47 Thunderbolt** (held over from this edition!) and we visit Andy Taylor at **C.T. Aviation,** the expert shipping company!

AVAILABLE MAY 31st 1992

Lance Aircraft Supply

THE PARTS SPECIALISTS IN SUPPLYING T-6, HARVARD AND SNJ SPARES

T-6 Owners are invited to come and see for yourself and browse through the Worlds Largest AT-6, Harvard and SNJ airframe spare parts inventory
This is our 23rd year in the T-6 parts business

LANCE AIRCRAFT SUPPLY, INC.
2246 Wisconsin Street P.O. Box 29205, Dallas, TX 75229 U.S.A.
Toll Free ORDER Desk 800 752 4005
Information and other calls (214) 247 3701

Round the World Invader

June 1992 marks the start of a very interesting event. The first Round-the-World air race is scheduled to leave Paris en route Helsinki - Moscow - Alaska - California-Washington-Canada-Greenland and Iceland. So far some 35 aircraft have entered for the event.

This includes two intrepid European pilots who plan to race A-26 N7079G/44-35562 in the event. Lady Barbel Abela, a German citizen living in London, and Len Perry, a U.K. based flying instructor from White Waltham, have entered the event in the Invader. The aircraft was purchased in Florida in November 1991 and flown to Brownsville, Texas, where it is being overhauled and repainted by *Southwind Aviation*, a facility with experience of warbird restoration and who specialise in DC-3 overhaul.

The A-26 was delivered to the USAF in May 1945 and served in a succession of units, the last of which was the 106th Tactical Reconnaissance Squadron, Night Photo, Air National Guard based at Birmingham Municipal Airport in Alabama. It was dropped from the USAF Inventory in April 1958.

Between 1958 and 1961 the aircraft went to On *Mark Engineering*, Van Nuys, California for conversion to On Mark Invader status. 1961 saw the aircraft being operated by the Texas Gas Transmission Corporation of Owensboro, Kentucky as N707TG. Ownership passed to Natrona Services Inc who operated the aircraft from 1969 to 1988. Natrona re-registered the aircraft as N7079G.

Conrad Yelvington acquired the aircraft in 1988 and it was purchased from a private owner in Florida by Barbel C. Abela in 1991.

Following overhaul at Southwind, the aircraft is being painted in an all black colour scheme with a snakes head nose, and after some flying in the USA it is planned to ferry the aircraft to the UK where it will be available for air show work prior to the air race commencing in mid-June. Once the race is complete (hopefully with

a victory under their belts) the Invader will again be available for air show work.

Not content with racing the Invader, Barbel and Len then plan to fly a Beech 18 from England to Australia in October this year as part of a vintage aircraft rally. The Beech 18 (which is a true C-45G) was discovered in a hangar in Saratoga, Wyoming where it had lain unflown for some 23 years. Total time on the airframe was 1970 hours; all radios and omnis are valve driven and work, as does the ADF coffee grinder. According to Len 'even the hydraulic

autopilot still works'. The machine had never been converted to cargo use. apart from three blade props the aircraft is totally original. Len successfully ferried the aircraft to *Blackhawk Airways*, Janesville, Wisconsin for a new annual and fitting of the spar strap modification. Another spectacular paint scheme is promised before the aircraft is delivered to the UK in the Spring or summer this year, prior to the air race.

Barbel also purchased Harvard IV G-BRLV in November (see WW15). named *Night Train* the aircraft was formerly owned by Lloyd Owens. It continues to be based at *The Squadron*, North Weald and some 50 hours have been flown on the machine in just two months. Needless to say Len is interested in hearing from potential sponsors for the A-26 and if anyone is interested in booking the aircraft for airshow appearances Len can be contacted on 0491 641757 or Fax 0491 641242, or you can write to *Bar-Belle Productions*, Cottage 4, Ewelme Down House, Ewelme, Oxfordshire OX10 6PQ.

Top: Beech 18 (a true C-45G) was flown to Blackhawk Airways at Janesville, Wisconsin, for a full overhaul and spar strap mod. **Left:** *The intrepid Invader pilots, Len Perry and Barbel Abela (Len Perry Photographs)*

C'est Magnifique!

Etchetto - the Skyraider is registered F-AZHK.
The Swiss Vampire auction has resulted in several DH-100s and DH-115s being imported to France. Though final details are being checked DH-100 J-1155 (c/n 664) was purchased by the *Musee de L'Air* at Le Bourget. DH-100 J-1178 (c/n687) belongs to Michel Pont(above photo by J. Guillem) who runs the *Savigny Les Beaunes Museum (Jets)* and should be kept in hot flying condition, operating from its base at Dijon!

Thierry Thomassin brings us up to date with all the latest happenings on the **French Warbird Scene**

There has been a significant amount of warbird activity in France since our last report. This has included a number of new aircraft being imported, including several major types.

Now famous for its Skyraider activities, the sixth Douglas AD-4N (Bu Aer 127002, ex SFERMA No.61 and ex TR-LQE) arrived here last January from Gabon(illustrated top right by J. Guillem). It was imported by Mr. Michele Gineste who has since unfortunately died. The aircraft will be operated from Le Havre in 1992 on behalf of the owner's family by Maurice

Another Vampire, serial J-1159 (c/n) 668) belongs to Gerard Marie-Berger. The aircraft has been fitted with an original nose section and repainted in French Air Force colours of unit EC 2/4 *Lafayette* Squadron and coded 4-LF with the serial VZ221; registered F-AZHJ, it made its first airshow appearance for the 75th anniversary of the *Escadrille* last October.

J-1199 belongs to a new association named

Atlantic and is based at Caen with the registration F-AZHH. Two other aircraft (serials not currently to hand) are based with *Amicale J.B. Salis* at Le Havre (and to be fitted with an original nose) and another with *Aero Spaciale* (Yves Duval) based at Rennes. Another DH-100 was purchased by Phillipe Denis.

DH-115s U-1229 (c/n 989) belongs to Messrs. Descamps, Carton and Goedraad and is registered F-AZGU, currently at Cannes-Mandelieu on the French Riviera. Yves Duval also has a DH-115 based at Rennes-St. Jaques (registered F-AZHU ex U-1210 c/n 870) along with another airframe.

Mr. Villa has two DH-115s based at Nimes and Philippe Denis also has another two aircraft located there.

Also on the French jet scene Sud Vatour IIN No.348 made its first civilian airshow appearance at La Fete Alais in 1991. It is the only one of its type in the world in airworthy condition and it is registered F-AZHP. This impressive jet is operated by CEV pilots and engineers who have flown it in military service and it is based at Bretigny. Another newcomer to the jet scene was the imported aero L-39 *Albatros* F-ZVLS belonging to Michel Bidoux which arrived at Tousus Le Noble last July. It has unfortunately been impounded by customs.

Noteworthy arrivals since our last report include North American B-25J 45-8811/N9621C (ex Harry Doan) which is operated by *Apache Aviation* based at Dijon. Also imported by the same company is the CAC 18 Mk 22 Mustang N286JB ex Victor Haluska of *Santa Monica Propeller*; this aircraft is coded JD-8 and named *The Best Years of Our Lives. Aero Trader* at Chino organised the shipping of the aircraft

France is also a haven for trainers, more particularly the T-6. Arriving in France last year was Canadian Car Foundry Harvard Mk IV C-FUVQ (CCF 4-128/construction number 20337) from Canada. It is now based at Etampes as F-AZIG. North American T-6G 49-3432 (c/n 168558 ex French Air Force) made its first flight after restoration from La Ferte Alais, registered F-AZGS. It is operated by the *Association D'Amateurs de Aero De Collection* - and based at Luneville.

The T-28 is also showing up in increasing numbers with the import of the ex Scandinavian T-28C Bu No 140547/N2800Q which was purchased by Monsieur Sporrer, an *Air Inter* Captain. It will be based at Toulouse Blagnac. Another T-28B Bu 138130 is registered N393W escaped the WW net when it was imported in 1990; it is owned by *Apache Aviation*.

Jacques Bourett's P-51D F-AZMU (Photo on page 48 lower by J. Guillem) has had a new Zeuschel Engines Merlin installed plus regular maintenance work following small operational mishap last year. **WW Thierry Thomassin**

Who can zeese be in ze back seat? Ze grin is zat of Thierry Thomassin in Aero Retro's T-6G F-AZBL looking immaculate in the French sun. Christian Martin is flying the aircraft (Top) by J. Guillem. Centre: Aero Retro's Yak 18 F-AZFG with J.M. Dursy at the controls - airborne from St. D'Albert Rambon in June last year (Thierry Thomassin photograph). Lower: Formerly with The Scandinavian Historic Flight T-28C N2800Q is seen here in October last year at Orly airport. (Jacques Guillem photograph).

Eastman Leather Clothing

In the 1990's quality is something that doesn't always seem to be around with some company's cutting corners and production costs in an effort to survive.

One company that produces goods where quality is the keyword in a very competetive market is *Eastman Leather Clothing* of Ivybridge, Devon, manufacturers of authentic replica flying jackets.

So where did all this start for Director Gary Eastman? From a very young age Gary was interested in aviation. By the age of 14 his interest turned to World War II and he began buying books on the subject. When he was 19 the interest developed into a fascination and Gary began attending military fairs and air shows where he found the acquisition of real aviation memorabilia most interesting. 'It was around this time that I bumped into my first original World War II type A-2 flying jacket. I was immediately enthralled with my find. It was what was associated most with those intrepid American flyers I had read so much about in the books. The look and smell of the old leather spoke a million words' enthused Gary.

In 1983 Gary ventured to the USA to do some travelling, all in all about six months of moving around the United States. During his travels he discovered some more original A-2s along with other types of jackets and paraphernalia.

Where did it go from here? 'Upon returning to the UK I found myself unemployed and was reluctantly forced to sell some of my jackets in order to get some money together. I found there was an overwhelming response to my advertisements for these jackets and sold them all within the week'.

It didn't take long for him to start thinking about the business of making some replica jackets -'I thought to myself, this would make a good business, if only I could get a constant supply? I contacted a few people I had got to know in the U.S.A. to see if they could locate some more jackets for me, but unfortunately nothing of any quantity was forthcoming'.

As time progressed and Gary investigated further, the situation developed. 'It was at this point that I pondered and imagined how fantastic it would be if I could reproduce these jackets as exact copies. I knew of a few other companies that had made half hearted attempts, but what if something was produced that was a *stitch for stitch* replica of the original? Exactly like the wartime versions?

After looking into the possibilities of undertaking a seemingly impossible task Gary finally produced his first A-2 jacket in July 1985. He sold it at a military fair to a Frenchman for £99.00. He was delighted! And so Eastman Leather Clothing was launched.

From then on things went from strength to strength. Within another 18 months not only could he not make enough A-2s to satisfy

demand, people began asking for other styles of wartime jackets - B-3s, RAF Sheepskin (Irvin type) and even Luftwaffe styles. So how did

Main picture: *Gary cutting out an A-2 from a hide. This steerhide or horsehide is specially tanned and finsihed to wartime specifications.* ***Above:*** *Detail shot of authentic buckle (nickel plated brass) - the right shape too! All fittings are specially made.*

Gary cope with the demand? 'Well, from here I moved into bigger premises and took on some skilled machinists to make other styles. It was soon clear that authenticity had to be the order of the day with every jacket being personally checked by myself before it leaves our premises'.

Before too long Gary was advertising his jackets in aviation publications and word of mouth

soon made *Eastman Leather Clothing* the company tp purchase a replica leather jacket from.

'Today we work on a 'made to order' basis here at *Eastman's*. We work from stock patterns which are made to the same specifications as the World War II garments. If somebody wants a jacket we make it specially for them. We have always had quite a queue and delivery is currently 12 weeks, although we can get that down to four weeks depending on how busy we are'.

Today it can be confusing for someone wanting to purchase a truly authentic reproduction World War II flying jacket. Much of the time they are unsure of what they should look for and what various parts of the jacket should look like. Of course many of the regular advertisements in trade publications boast that theirs is the most authentic garment. When we asked Gary about this he replied 'Anyone can say "this jacket is the most authentic", but proving it is another matter. I guarantee the *Eastman* range of flying jackets as the most authentic, anywhere, and am very happy to show details of original garments in our colour catalogue for people to compare. As a collector myself I would not allow anything less than absolute authenticity in my jackets'.

Quite a claim you might say, and when I questioned Gary further he said 'We have gone to a great deal of expense to reproduce each detail with the optimum amount of accuracy, right down to the shape and style of buckles, zip pulls, fasteners etc. We don't just use stock materials from suppliers and say "that's close enough" like many other companies, who then turn around and tell a potential customer "this is completely authentic", but we do it properly'.

One cannot be anything but impressed with Gary's philosophy in this respect and it is quite amazing to see large numbers of people wearing his A2 and other style jackets.

Eastman Leather currently produce replica jackets as follows: Type A-2 intermediate flying jacket (leather), the Type B-3 winter flying jacket (Sheepskin), the Type ANJ-4 (sheepskin), the RAF Irvin sheepskin flying jacket, the USN G-1 intermediate leather flying jacket (reviewed in Warbirds Worldwide 19), the black Luftwaffe (private purchase design, leather), RAF 1936 pattern flying boots and type B-2 gunners cap (sheepskin).

Further details of the full range of *Eastman Leather Clothing* can be obtained by contacting: **Eastman Leather Clothing, Ivybridge, Devon PL21 9AB. Telephone (0752) 896874 or Fax (0752 690579). In the United States Nose Art Unlimited at 100 Heritage Road, Maple Shade, NJ 08052 should be contacted on (609) 234 9147.**
WW Paul Coggan

This is a copy of the private purchase Luftwaffe jacket you see in many wartime photographs. There were actually several styles and this is one of them. Below: The authentic linen label in the RAF jacket. This is how they really were. Black print on white linen, not shiny satin!

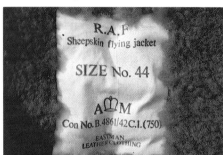

R.A.F
Sheepskin flying jacket

SIZE No. 44

A⚜M
Con No.B.4861/42C.I.(750)
EASTMAN
LEATHER CLOTHING

The Eastman Leather Clothing A-2 jacket, made in two colours (as it was in World War II) is still the company's best selling jacket and most popular line. With the 50th Anniversary of the U.S. Forces arrival in 1942 this year there is bound to be an even bigger demand than usual for this style. (All photographs courtesy Eastman Leather Clothing.)

NEW PRODUCTS

Introduction

In the future, this book review column will be a regular item in *Warbirds Worldwide*, and we aim to bring you news and reviews of the latest releases of interest to readers. We also hope to cover a classic book or series each issue, bringing books that are of interest but may no longer be available to your attention. Above and beyond that we will scour lists for books that we believe owners, operators and enthusiasts will find of use and we will attempt to give an opinion on each. We will try to bring you book news of books in preparation, and people needing help with compiling information. If you wish to bring a book to our attention, or have a request for help please write to us at WW Books, P.O. Box 99, Mansfield, Notts. NG19 9GU - WW James Kightly(JK) & Gary Brown (GB)

Book News

The book on the well known U.K. Boeing B17G G-BEDF *Sally* B that was to come from *Aston Press* has been delayed indefinitely, and may now not appear at all, which would be pity. Graham Warner, prime mover behind the Blenheim restoration at Duxford, and author of *The Forgotten Bomber* (reviewed in WW18) is preparing what should be the definitive work in the Blenheim's history, and he would appreciate any information or photographs that could add to this work. Please write direct to *The Aircraft Restoration Company*, Building 66, I.W.M. Duxford, Cambridgeshire, CB2 4QR, England. I am sure all material will be treated with the greatest care. Elsewhere in this section is a review of Jeff Ethell and Robert Sand's *Fighter Command* as well and an article by Jeff on the same subject will appear in a later edition. He is also preparing a book to cover the Royal Air Force in the same way, and anyone with wartime colour shots of R.A.F. aircraft is urged to get in touch with Jeff at the following address: R.1 Box 3154, Front Royal, VA 22630, USA. The thought of the R.A.F. getting the same treatment as the U.S.A.A.F. is almost too good to be true!

Jeff's book on the American's in Europe is, however by no means alone, and though each treads a slightly different path, and we aim to cover some of the others in future issues. Worth looking out for now though, are *War Paint: Fighter Nose Art of WWII*, *The History of Aircraft Nose Art*, *Fighters of the Mighty Eighth*, *Hell Bent For Leather: The Story of the A-2 & G-1 flight jackets* and *Fighters of the Mighty Eighth 1942-45*.

The Reviews

Squadron/Signal books are a well established

coming from Texas and available in the U.K. through the Octopus Distribution, the people responsible for O*sprey* books. The series follows a set format of a 50 page soft cover landscape layout with cover paintings by Don Greer (who is also responsible for the centrespread colour profiles). They are aimed mainly at modellers, each major modification to the aircraft being covered by good quality line drawings.

Though there is a basic amount of text, serving to delineate the history of the type, the major asset to the series is the range of black and white photographs. These are often taken from unlikely sources and private collections, always making these books worth examining for reference. Several major warbird types have been covered in the past. Finally the price is extremely good value at £6.50 in the U.K.

In Action Series No.117

Hawker Sea Fury in Action Ron Mackay Squadron/Signal Publications ISBN 0897472675 £6.50

The cover almost inevitably features the 9th August 1952 combat between Lt. Charmichael and a North Korean MiG 15, the painting as ever being well executed by Don Greer. The back cover features a Royal Australian Navy FB11 in the aerobatic team colours made famous in more recent years by VH-HFX and the U.S. based N21SF. The caption refers to it merely as an Australian Sea Fury, missing the reason for the overall blue scheme. The other back cover scheme is T20 VX280, the first production example.

The book cover the development, production and service history of the type, the second part of the book covering the foreign users, in good detail. The colour centre spread consists of profiles of various Sea Furies, including the prototype, and aircraft from Canada, Burma, Holland, Iraq, Cuba, Pakistan and an example of the well known German TT20s. The last section of the book has a few photos of preserved Sea Furies, rich ground these days, but badly served here. Despite the recent nature of the pictures, they are murky and undistinguished, being of little use and no pleasure to look at. There are photos of R.N.H.F. TF 956, Mike Carrol's N878M, VH-BOU, N232, N51SF Cottonmouth, NX20SF Dreadnought and G-FURY, Despite the opportunity for a rich choice of colour, none have been chosen for Don's paintings. I cannot recommend any of these photos, and considering these aircraft have had long and extremely public careers there is no excuse for the poor quality of the pictures. The drawings supplied throughout the book are good, and illustrate the changes to the airframes very well, though they all suffer from a mystery line in the cowling that I suspect is a camouflage demarcation line carried in error. Despite these criticisms, the book gives good value for money, and serves to illustrate the variety of schemes the Sea Fury has worn in mil-

itary service. We will return to this series in the future.**JK**

Fighter Command
American Fighters in Original WWII Colour
Jeffrey Ethell and Robert T Sand
Motorbooks International U.S $ 29.95, Haynes U.K. £18.95

Suddenly there seems to be glut of books dealing with the U.S. Air Forces of WWII. The good news is that most of them seem to cover areas previously untouched or little dealt with.

Fighter Command, as the subtitle says, is all about U.S. Fighters in colour and the selection of photographs is excellent, taking the reader from Stateside training through the Mediterranean Theatre and northwest Europe right up to the end of the war where the fighters were being cut up by German civilian labour.

Many books in this field concentrate on good (or useful) photos of the aircraft to the exclusion of all else. This doesn't, and I think it adds to the richness of the book, giving the reader that elusive feel of what it was like to be there. The M.T.O. shots are something else, William Skinners Spitfire Mk.VIII *Lonesome Polecat* getting star treatment, but some of the most interesting aircraft covered are the captured e/a; a Macchi MC202 Folgore renamed *Wacky Macky* and adorned with U.S. insignia, as is a Messerschmitt Bf109, and an unnamed Italian trainer flown by the enlisted men of the 308th Sqn. The shots taken in north-west Europe cover the gamut of the fighter pilot and ground crew's life, the freezing winter days and hot harvest summers coming to life in the colour photos. The relief of being back after a long-range escort mission is shown in several shots, as is the elation of a successful sortie. Shots of a Cletrac tractor in the mud and airmen piling up bright silver drops tanks also bring these mundane scenes full to life.

Though entitled *Fighter Command*, and covering the obvious P-51, P-47, and P-38's it does not exclude all else; U.S. bombers appear, as do F-5 Lightnings and a section on German aircraft seen on captured bases, even a lowly *Shagbat* (Supermarine Walrus) creeps in on page 19, while page 100 has a very special Mustang: 12193WW.

If this review gives the impression that the book is all photos, that would be quite wrong; they are well supported by the text, which consists of reminiscences from all types of personnel involved with these forces; the obvious pilots (from Aces to junior aircrew) ground crew, and the ever popular Red Cross personnel and civilians. Though the text suffers from a few typos, this is a well produced read on good quality glossy paper, and defines the best sort of coffee table book. Though some shots are oddly cropped and a *very few* are unsharp, most are first class, and each photo has a good reason for it's inclusion; theres is no padding at all. Fighter Command comes thoroughly recommended.

8th Air Force Bomber Stories
Ian McLachlan & Russell J.Zorn
Patrick Stephens Limited
ISBN 1852603674 £17.50

The well timed release of this book to coincide with the fiftieth anniversary of the Eighth Air Force's arrival in the U.K. highlights the terrifying nature of the war.

This book is divided into over 40 separate chapters, each covering just one incident that befell the crew of a bomber. When one thinks of 8th Air Force operations, we immediately associate them with high level formations avoiding flak and fighters in daylight operations, protected by an entourage of *little friends*. In this book the authors graphically show how many aircraft were lost to other technical malfunctions, crew inexperience and downright misfortune, which were almost as much of a problem as AA fire and enemy fighter operations. The backbone of the book is the vast collection of crash pictures taken by Russell J Zorn who was a U.S.A.A.F. photographer based at Honnington with the 1st Strategic Air Depot. His duties included photographing the many crash sites in the locality, and from this core of photographs crews were traced and locations revisited to determine a true picture of each incident. Where possible local people still living in the area have been interviewed recalling faded memories of the end of stricken bombers. Sometimes this work has determined the cause for an unexplained crash from almost fifty years ago.

This work gives the true picture of 8th Air Force ops where dangers were an ever present risk, and shows what happens when your luck runs out, very different from the Hollywood type image depicted in film like *Memphis Belle*. The next time you see a reenactment of a staged dogfight at a display or in a feature film, just remember the crews who did not pull out of a terminal dive or survive an undercarriage hang-up, for in reality, it was many rather than few. **GB**

Spitfire: A Living Legend
Jeremy Flack
Osprey ISBN 0850456193. £10.99

Though no longer new, this book is well worthy of a mention, having been an excellent summary of the state of Spitfire preservation for when it came out seven years ago in 1985! The coverage is good, dealing with Spitfires both active and under restoration. Several aircraft have changed hands or schemes since, and as a result the book serves as a snapshot of the Spitfire scene in 1985, the balance being of photographs taken especially for the book. At least one photo of a Spitfire under restoration I saw recently had a copy of this book spread open on the wing, and I can think of no

better recommendation than that. What we need now is a new Spitfire book; the good news being Osprey have another coming in May this year: *Spitfire: The Legend Lives On*. This also is from Jeremy Flack, and given the good job he did first time around, I for one anticipate an excellent work; as the cliche has it "watch this space"JK

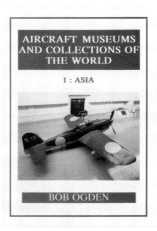

AIRCRAFT MUSEUMS & COLLECTIONS OF THE WORLD: Vol. 1: *ASIA*
Bob Ogden
Bob Ogden Publications
ISBN 1 873854 00 5 £4.50 plus P&P

If you want a potted but nevertheless interesting and fascinating tour around the world's air museums on the lowest possible budget then Bob Ogden has the answer with the first in a series of indispensible books covering the subject.

As Bob's introduction points out, this is the first in a series which will eventually cover all the museums in the world. Museums are being established at a great rate and constant research is necessary in order to keep the work accurate. Reading through the book is like looking at jewels in a hereto undiscovered cache. The book is black and white throughout and the photographic coverage is good - giving a real glimpse at some of the static machines that hopefully one day will take to the air again. No doubt the entire series will become collector's items and I am full of praise for Bob's obvious dedication in preparing it. At first glance you might just think this is a book that you won't sit and read cover to cover. However, pick it up and I guarantee you will not be able to put it down in a hurry. An excellent guide for everyone interested in warbirds and other vintage aircraft, whether you travel on dedicated aircraft searching trips or just escape briefly from the wife on a foreign foray. One that will stay close to me...... Buy It! **PC**

Available from Bob Ogden Publications, 13 Western Avenue, Woodley, Berkshire, ENGLAND RG5 3BJ at just £4.95 plus postage.

As the first in our series of classic works we turn to the sadly no longer available book *Airborne* by Neil Williams. Though published in hardback in 1977 and now long out of print, it can still be found on second hand stalls and

specialist booksellers always try to obtain copies. (Please don't pester Airlife with requests however) Some of the text appeared previously in magazines, notably *Pilot*, but the narrative of the book is better than the snippets that this format presented. The book is illustrated by Neil's wife Lynn Williams, and the superb black and white drawings bring the text even more to life. Lynn is responsible for the illustration of another book; *Aerobatics* but that's another story...

Airborne Neil Williams
Airlife, now out of print ISBN 095045432X

The name Neil Williams is as familiar today as it was at the time of his death in 1977. Whenever a Spitfire displays the older cadre of enthusiasts always compare it to the graceful displays that Neil performed in the Mk.IX MH434, then owned by Adrian Swire or the Mk.V AR501. His displays were the highlight of airshows nationwide, and it is fitting that *Airborne* should open with an account of his first flight in a Spitfire.

After learning to fly in Wales, the Canadian born Williams joined the R.A.F. and was trained as a pilot in Canada. The book gives an insight into various memorable incidents that occurred and sometimes where a lesson was learnt the hard way! Among the warbird types that Neil had flown and recounted in *Airborne* are the deHavilland Mosquito, Hawker Hunter, Casa 2111, Gloster Meteor, Lockheed T33, E.E. Canberra and of course the Spitfire.

As a former pupil of the *Empire Test Pilot's School*, Williams was tasked with flying a wide range of types with often only pilot's notes available for familiarisation. It was with this background that he was requested to fly the aircraft of the *Shuttleworth Collection*. Some of these machines have what is best described as very marginal performances and sometimes are strictly limited to straight hops. This was so for Britain's oldest flying original aircraft, the 1912 Blackburn Monoplane. Williams was so encouraged by the veteran's performance during these hops across the airfield that he chose to take full responsibility of performing a circuit for the first time in many years. It is his enthusiasm and confidence that echo throughout the pages of this book.

Despite several near fatal accidents, which include a dramatic display accident at Biggin Hill (causing the commentators immortal line"He's taken it behind the hangar.... and left it there!) and a wing failure in a Zlin during practice for the 1970 *World Aerobatic Championships*, Williams love of flying did not diminish whether he was aviating a Bristol Boxkite around Old Warden or diving at supersonic speed in a Hawker Hunter. Essential for all enthusiasts and budding display pilots the authors narrative describes the uncompromising nature of flight. **GB**

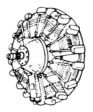

Lake Schwerin's *Dora Nine*

Mark Sheppard & Axel Urbanke detail the recovery of a Luftwaffe Fw190-D9 from Lake Schwerin

Lake Schwerin's secret unveiled. The centre fuselage section of the Fw190 is lifted from the water under the watchful eye of a police launch. The bottom hatch of the water methanol tank is missing. Note the black and white home defence bands of JG26 (Axel Urbanke)

The person responsible for rediscovering the wreck of the Fw190 Dora Nine (unknown Werke No.) white / ? of I Gruppe/1 Staffel JG26 was Axel Urbanke. In 1986, whilst conducting research for a book-about III / JG54 (IV/JG26), II/JG26 and I/JG 26 in 1944-45, he read about a Focke Wulf 190 D9 aircraft being lost in Lake Schwerin on April 17th 1945.

The loss of the aircraft was confirmed by a reunion of ex JG26 pilots who also stated this aircraft was lost toward the end of the war. A local angler by the name of Georg Diecke also helped in locating the aircraft (either from being on the lake or from losing his line whilst fishing in the lake.) Because the Fw190 was lost in the final stages of the war the Luftwaffe did not recover the machine.

Several other aircraft were lost in the lake due to air combat action that took place in this area, but these were lifted in 1945-1946 by the Russians for scrap. The team only had a rough idea of where the aircraft was lost; from combat reports they knew the aircraft was heading south-westerly for Sulte and that it was lost in the northernmost lake of the two.

So this rare machine remained undisturbed and is the subject of this article. It was probably the last remaining aircraft in a restorable state; other crashes into the water hit with a much harder impact causing the machines to break up. Because lake Schwerin was (until recently) in East Germany and with there being

no diving clubs the aircraft remained undisturbed for 45 years.

After finding out about the aircraft in 1986, Axel Urbanke informed Mr Gunter Leonhardt (who is a major benefactor of the *Luftwaffen Museum at Uetersen*). Due to the political difference between East and West Germany at the time no search or recovery was possible. This all changed when the Berlin Wall came down and Germany was united. In the summer of 1990 with changes happening in Eastern Europe so quickly it was decided to recover the aircraft as soon as possible before it was recovered by someone else.

By going through German combat reports the aircraft's whereabouts was roughly determined within the confines of the quite substantial lake; Made up of two 'pools', each about 6 by 2.5 miles in size. On the 12th November 1990 the recovery team started their sweep of the northern lake. With the help of *Firma Nautik Keppler sonar* the two parts of the fuselage were located in 20m (65 feet) of water. Pictures of the main body helped to determine the state it was in and helped decide the best way of recovering it.

On the morning of the 15th November the

recovery team lifted the first section of the fuselage out of the water for the first time after being submerged in the lake for just over 45 years and 7 months. On the first recovery in November the fuselage, engine and tail were recovered. Initially, the wings were not located and a further expedition was planned to recover them. Eventually, in January 1991 they were recovered. Mr. Gunter Leonhardt used experience gained from recovering four Junkers Ju52's from the Hatvigvansee in Norway. Using lifting bags to recover the airframes to the surface and a crane to bring it ashore the recovery went well.

The Fw190 was in four main pieces, with the wings having sheared off at the wing spar attachments to the fuselage; largely due to the high speed impact with the water. These were recovered about 100 yards from the main body in a separate recovery operation.

The main fuselage had broken in half on the line of the number eight frame member just behind the cockpit. The engine in turn was buried nose down in about six feet of mud up to the cockpit's armoured windscreen. The only dismantling involved was the separation of the tail from the rear fuselage at the point where the extended box section to the fuselage was

Lake Schwerin *Dora Nine*

The rear tail section ashore with the tail wheel off its axle from the impact with the water. This part of the aircraft was dismantled from the fuselage whilst under water (Axel Urbanke)

added for the long nosed FW190's. This was done under water with the tail being raised separately. When the aircraft was ashore the extent of preservation could be seen clearly. The best part of the aircraft was undoubtedly the Junkers V12 213-A2 engine and the surrounding panels. It was this, along with the camouflage paint that was extremely well preserved. The MG 131 machine guns above the engine and the cockpit area were in good condition as most of it had all been protected by the fine silt on the lake bed.

The green upper and grey/blue lower camouflage on the engine was clearly noticeable and even the red coolant level stencilling was crisp on the upper panels next to the 13mm gun ports. Steel that normally rusts quite quickly had survived in the mud especially the exhausts and machine gun barrels. Even the propeller hub survived the high speed impact though the (V9) wide paddle bladed wooden propeller did not. The black spinner with its white spiral (this was a requirement towards the end of 1944) is plainly evident and was in good condition considering the impact. Though the main body of the aircraft was relatively complete a lot of the smaller hatch covers to the cannons and fuselage bay were lost.

Areas of the camouflage and markings were clearly recognisable as the main aircraft was recovered, especially the swastika on the fin and the black/white *Defence of the Reich* band of JG26 to the rear fuselage of the aircraft where it had been separated from the tail. The wings took the brunt of the impact and were in a bad condition, with the skins being corroded and covered in mussels.

The lower skins on the wing tips buckled up, when the aircraft hit the water. Generally the wings were also badly distorted and in a worse condition than the fuselage.

After visiting the *Luftwaffen Museum* at Uetersen

in July and getting permission to see the remains in a locked hangar it was plain to see the task facing the restoration team.

All the instruments and major internal parts have been removed and labelled to help preserve items from further deterioration. The aircraft was still in five main parts. The restoration will involve nearly all new skins throughout with most stringers and floating ribs requiring replacement. Undoubtedly it was the engine that was in the best condition and this was removed from the *Luftwaffen Museum* by Mr. Gunter Leonhardt who is now restoring it. This will then probably be put on display until the main Dora Nine restoration is undertaken. This is a long term and costly project and when the main aircraft restoration is completed the engine will again be installed in the fuselage. They hope to have it totally restored by the end of 1992, or early 1993.

Besides this the Director of the *Luftwaffen Museum*, Oblt. Dr. Dieter Rogge needs help in locating Fw190 parts (in any condition). Also, any technical assistance or information that would help him with the restoration of this important and rare World War II German aircraft would be most appreciated.

Though it will never return to flying condition because it is deemed to be too valuable, it will be restored to a full military specification and put on static display similar to the Bf109 G2 *Gustav* that is in the middle of a total rebuild at the museum now and should be finished in the near future.

Only one other FW190 D9 is thought to have survived out of an estimated 650-700 built as well as a D13 (and not including the Ta-142 HO that is in storage awaiting restoration at the *Paul E.Garber Facility* at Silver Hill in Maryland). Five D9s were thought to have been taken to the United States during and after the end of the war for evaluation. Of these the whereabouts

of Werke Nmrs. 210079, 211016 (originally thought to have been 210016 though this aircraft was lost on the 29/12/44 during service with III/JG54 (Oblt. Bellaire killed), 401392 and 600651 are unknown; though they are thought to have been scrapped.

The survivor is Fw190 D9 Werke No.601088/FE-120 that belongs to the *National Air and Space Museum* but is on loan to Wright Patterson AFB at Dayton Ohio. This is in the colours of IV 9 Sturm)/JF3. The other that was a later mark with heavier armament and a different engine is the FW190 featured in *Warbirds Worldwide* No.12. This is a D13 Werke No. 174013 / 836017/FE-118 which started re-equipping JG 26 after the war though only a few units received them before the conclusion of hostilities. This survivor has just been fully restored and is at the *Champlin Fighter Museum* in the colours of Yellow 10 of I Gruppe/3 Staffel/JG26.

With the demise of the Iron Curtain further aircraft recoveries have already commenced. Whilst researching information on this aircraft I managed to find out about a further two D9s being lost on Lake Schwerin on May 1st 1945 as well as another D9 on Binenwalde Lake on 20th April 1945. It is known that there was heavy aerial fighting in this central part of Germany in 1945 because of the shrinking area in which the Germans were operating. Also Sulte Airfield (from where this D9 operated) was right next to the lake and of course a target for marauding Allied aircraft. What is exceptional about this particular aircraft is that it survived in the lake until 1990. Most of the other aircraft which included Soviet types, were *supposedly* lifted for scrap in the 1940s by the Russians. These three losses were found after looking through fragmented records of only a few RAF squadrons operating in the area of old East Germany that has twenty main lakes, so if this one survived then the chances of further aircraft surviving seems reasonable. Several aircraft were lost in the last few months of World War II especially by the Germans and there must be numerous wreckage from crash sites existing within Germany, Poland, Russia and elsewhere. It is exciting to think about the prospect of further German aircraft as well as Russian and Allied lend - lease types being recovered and restored.

Hopefully over the next few years we will be able to report the recovery of more of these aircraft. The possibility of having a Fw190 flying by it's 50th anniversary in 1994 is possible. (It reached the fighter units to become a front line fighter in 1944). It is known that further rare aircraft are being located in remote areas of Russia's lakes and forests. Some of are complete and generally well preserved. So though this article is a departure for *Warbirds Worldwide* we strongly believe that this source of rare aircraft has yet to be explored further - the resources available to the majority of our restoration companies are such that even the